The Sacred Art

The Sacred Art

Preaching & Theology
in the African American Tradition

Olin P. Moyd

Judson Press ® Valley Forge

The Sacred Art: Preaching & Theology
in the African American Tradition
© 1995
Judson Press, Valley Forge, PA 19482-0851

Bible quotations in this volume are from the New Revised Standard Version of the Bible, copyright 1989 by the Division of Christian Education of the National Council of the Churches of Christ in the U.S.A. Used by permission. All rights reserved. (NRSV); *The New Testament in Modern English*, Rev. ed. Copyright © J. B. Phillips 1972. Used by permission of The Macmillan Company and Geoffrey Bles, Ltd. (Phillips); the Revised Standard Version of the Bible, copyright © 1946, 1952, 1971, by the Division of Christian Education of the National Council of the Churches of Christ in the USA. Used by permission. (RSV); *The Holy Bible*, King James Version. (KJV)

Library of Congress Cataloging-in-Publication Data
Moyd, Olin P.
    The sacred art : preaching and theology in the African American tradi-
tion / by Olin P. Moyd.
        p. cm.
    Includes bibliographical references.
    ISBN 0-8170-1220-6
    1. Afro-American preaching. 2. Afro-American churches.
3. Theology, Practical. I. Title.
BV4208.U6M693 1995
251′.0089′96073—dc20   94-40270

Printed in the U.S.A.
95 96 97 98 99 00 01 02 8 7 6 5 4 3 2

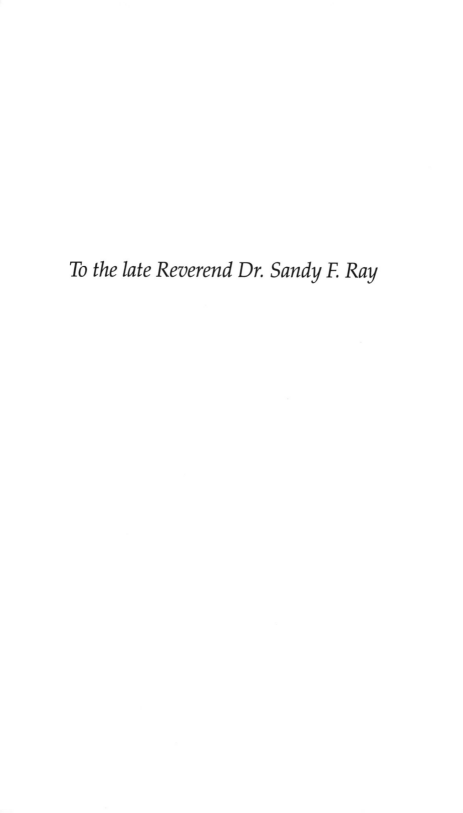

To the late Reverend Dr. Sandy F. Ray

Contents

Foreword

In the black community the church remains the center of life, educationally, spiritually, politically, and culturally. Many persons have hardly any education at all except what they learned in the church from the preachers. The faith that propels their lives and carries them step-by-step through the shadowy valleys and over wearisome mountains was generated in the church under the proclamations of the preacher. The commentaries of the preacher on political issues give guidance and focus for informed participation. And, in a diverse and multicultural environment, the preacher separates the trivial from the essential, shows where ethnic differences are important and should be preserved, and where such differences are inconsequential and should recede in favor of a larger community. Many are the burdens that the preacher must shoulder.

But this volume invites us to take an even closer look at the preacher and how he or she practices this unique calling. The writer has had a long and close familiarity with the most influential among the black clergy. He has heard their rhythmic, thunderous, humorous, folksy, ecstatic, impelling, ethereal messages. He has been active in their convention circles and involved in their leadership contests and political machinations. He has seen them at their best with the mantle of Elijah draped about them, and, sadly, at their most vulnerable moments, following the Master from afar. They are human.

With that advantage, we are privileged to enter into an intimate dialogue with the author as he exposes the black preacher microscopically. The traditional preaching, "telling the story," is a special focus of this work, but beyond that exercise, which, quite frankly, can often become simply theatrical and exploitative, the author carries us into an exploration of black theology.

How fortunate we would be if the gift of "telling the story" could be used to convey also the strong emphases of black theology, bringing the gospel to bear upon the conditions of black people and of the nation as a whole. Black theology is no more than a corrective for omissions and misplaced emphases in "other" theology. All theology should be good theology for all persons, but for so long theology spoke in soft, accommodating, dialect tones allowing the believers to be "at ease in Zion." The clarion call to justice by the prophets and the transparent, sincere discipleship to which Jesus invited us have been muffled and obscured. This book is a testimony to the black preachers, who—when at their best— are peerless in "telling the story" and calling us to Christian praxis.

Samuel D. Proctor
Pastor Emeritus, Abyssinian Baptist Church
New York City
Professor Emeritus, Graduate School of Education
Rutgers University

Preface

The sacred art of preaching and theology has been the hallmark in the African American worship tradition. This sacred art may be summed up as preaching theology.

Preaching and practical theology is the exploration of a new region in black theology. Preaching and practical theology are two sides of the same coin in the African American church and worship tradition. Practical theology is actualized in the life of the people rather than just verbalized in the classrooms of the academies. Practical theology is church theology that reflects upon the divine mandate for ministries of the church.

Practical theology has been the basic content in African American preaching, and preaching has been the vehicle of practical theology. The pastor-preacher-theologians have been the medium of transmitting theological truths to the masses in the African American communities. The pastor-preacher-theologians are those who provide the major theological interpretations for the masses of people, usually in church settings through their preaching.

The preachers have been engaged in interpretation and proclamation. The preaching has been the hallmark of hope and the pivot of promise for a pilgrim people. This admirable preaching tradition provided divine corrections and gave eternal directions to a people standing, at moments in human history, with their backs against the wall.

This is not intended to be a book on the "how to" of preaching and practical theology, but rather it is an attempt to show how preaching and practical theology has been done by master African American preachers. I will also point out the possibilities and the potentials of African American preaching and practical theology for the successors to this important tradition.

I have culled excerpts from many sermons of African American preacher-theologians. The purpose is to illustrate the form and content of African American preaching and practical theology. The appendix is a full manuscript of the late Reverend Dr. Sandy F. Ray. This sermon is a classical model of African American preaching that transmits a practical theology. It is a classical model of practical theology in that, while it deals with matters of eternal significance, it also deals with the divine mandate for the practical task of the church and its ministry to persons in their social context of existence.

African American women have made a tremendous contribution to the development of African American religion and churches. I have in my possession some of the manuscripts from *Those Preachin' Women*. I have included excerpts from their sermons in my illustrations.

Both the term "black" and the term "African American" are being used in reference to people in America of African descent. The term "black" is used mostly to reflect the term used in the historical period of the incidents to which I am making reference (example: chapter 2). The term "African American" is used to reflect the term being used to refer to Americans of African descent at the time of this writing.

This manuscript has evolved out of my study and experience as a pastor-theologian—being the theologian to a congregation in a pastoral setting, serving in an inner-city context for three decades—and as an academic theologian—teaching theology as adjunct faculty member in an academic setting for more than two decades.

This book will be most helpful to African American pastors and preachers who are responsible for perpetuating the African American preaching tradition. It will be useful for students in seminaries and Bible colleges who want to learn from the tradition of the masters. This book should be profitable reading for those who hear preaching. Our white brothers and sisters who read this book will discover what it is that has kept the African American churches alive, vibrant, and empowered.

In the chapters that follow, I will examine and explore several aspects of preaching and practical theology. Chapter 1 is a general introduction, discussing the problem, importance of the study, and limitations.

In chapter 2, I have surveyed the history of black theology. I believe that this background study is important for the understanding of this extension of the exploration of the black theological enterprise. Practical theology and practical preaching is discussed in chapter 3. Here I have also discussed the object and effect of practical theology and practical preaching.

While preaching the whole counsel of God is a task no human being is capable of completing, it has been a basic aspiration in African American preaching. This is the focus of chapters 4 and 5.

In chapter 6, I try to show how practical preaching in the African American community has empowered the people. The redemption motif in the sermons empowered the people to swim against the tide and to engage creatively in the redemptive movement.

Celebration is an integral part of the African American worship tradition. This celebration has roots in the Bible and in the African tradition. Celebration is also a major aspect in African American preaching. This is the matter discussed in chapter 7. I concluded with the discussion of "The Future of the God We Preach" in chapter 8. The God who will be known in the future is dependent upon the God that we preach today. It is not blasphemous to speak of the future of God since, by the Almighty's own divine plan, God chose to be revealed through preaching. The God who will be known to the masses in the future will not be limited to the God who is defined through theological treatises in the academy. The God of the future will be the God proclaimed to the people in the pew by the pastor-theologians.

As in all of my undertakings in my lifetime, I have had the unstinting help of a cadre of persons who care about my achievements. Since my publication of *Redemption in Black Theology*, many of my colleagues and friends have been encouraging me to write another major book, which has led to this publication.

I give special thanks to my indefatigable secretary, (Julia) Deloris Mack, for the production, reproduction, and corrections of this manuscript. I am greatly indebted to Lydia A. Brown and my administrative assistant, Hazel W. Davis, for their diligence in proofreading the manuscript. My appreciation is extended to

Bessie McKnight and the late Rajesh Mangatoo for their assistance in this production.

The Reverend Drs. James Fuller and Walter Thomas reviewed and critiqued the entire manuscript. Their comments are deeply appreciated and were very helpful for the improvement of the quality of the book. The comments of Bishop James B. Thornton on my discussion of the Holy Spirit in chapter 5 were helpful and are graciously appreciated.

I alone take full responsibility for the weaknesses of this work.

At the eleventh hour, I asked the Reverend Dr. Samuel D. Proctor to review the manuscript and to write the "Foreword," and he kindly consented to do so, for which I offer my thanks.

Over the years, my students have been the sounding boards and the inquisitors who have forced me to sharpen my focus on theology and preaching. To them I extend my gratitude. The Ecumenical Institute of Theology, St. Mary's Seminary and University in Baltimore, has provided the academic arena in which I have been privileged to teach and to develop these important themes of preaching and practical theology over the last two decades. I have also been privileged to teach preaching at the United Baptist College and Seminary of the United Baptist Missionary Convention in Baltimore since 1990. My colleagues in pastoral ministry have also provided me with many opportunities to preach and to teach in their congregations.

My wife, Marie, and my children and grandchildren have greatly encouraged me. They have also been generous in giving me uninterrupted time—that I should have spent with them—to pursue this project.

The ministers, officers, and members of the Mount Lebanon Baptist Church have been generous and supportive. They have always provided the atmosphere and the opportunity for me to pursue various projects.

Olin P. Moyd
Baltimore, Maryland
1994

Chapter 1

Introduction

Many and varied are the interpretations dealing with the teachings and the life of Jesus of Nazareth. But few of these interpretations deal with what the teachings and the life of Jesus have to say to those who stand, at a moment in human history, with their backs against the wall. To those who need profound succor and strength to enable them to live in the present with dignity and creativity, Christianity often has been sterile and of little avail.[1]

Interpretation and Proclamation

These truths were first proclaimed by the late mystic, scholar, and theologian Howard Thurman at the annual convocation on preaching at the School of Theology, Boston University, in 1935. The title of the lecture was "Good News for the Disinherited." The disinherited of which Thurman spoke were the African Americans who had been disenfranchised by the majority of Euro-Americans who claimed to be predominantly Christians. The content of the Euro-American theology and preaching had little to say to those whose backs were against the wall. But the interpretations and proclamations of the gospel in the African American churches gave special attention to the conditions and aspirations of a people who were denied the fulfillment of the American dream of liberty and justice for all.

Throughout African American history, the church has been the central public institution in the community. The preachers have been the central figures in their churches. Preaching has been the primary element in their worship. And practical theology has been the content and essence in their preaching.

Practical theology is church theology that is a reflection upon the divine mandate for the practical tasks of the church. These tasks include preaching, worship, education, counseling, pastoral care, church administration, church structure, all ministries, moral theology, and ethics. My primary focus in this book will be a reflection upon the task of preaching, which is just one region in the field of practical theology.

It was through preaching that the practical, everyday life concerns of the ordinary folk were addressed. This attention to the God-concern for the well-being of people gave rise to the tremendous growth and development of African American churches and denominations.

The God-consciousness that was promoted through the church reached every hamlet of African Americans. This means that the guiding principles, moral values, and sense of the sacred, even among the nonchurched, were shaped by the preaching and practical theology of the church. Some members of the household or the family transmitted these religious values among the nonchurched as well as among the churched. This tradition is not as prevalent today as it was two or three decades ago. Today we have in the African American communities second and even third generations of families who are nonchurched and are not greatly influenced by the African American church tradition—its spiritual and moral values. Thus, we need to reinforce the African American preaching tradition that greatly influenced the nonchurched as well as the churched in the past.

Historic African American preaching was both interpretation and proclamation, which is theology and preaching. It was interpreting and unraveling the whole counsel—the whole will and the whole plan—of God in the midst of the tribulations of the people and declaring or proclaiming that God would redeem them from their states and circumstances as well as from their sins and guilt. These interpretations were akin to that of Philip, who had an encounter with the Ethiopian eunuch, the treasurer of Queen Candace. Upon being directed by the Spirit, Philip got in the chariot with this visitor to Jerusalem, discovered that he was reading from the prophet Isaiah (Isaiah 53:7-8), and asked whether he needed help with interpretation. Upon consent, Philip took the passage from Isaiah and preached Jesus.

This court official was converted and baptized through Philip's interpretation and proclamation—his theology and preaching (Acts 8:26-38).

What was true in the Lukan narrative is also true in the African American preaching traditions. Even today in our more literate society, when it comes to matters of spiritual transcendency, eternal truths, and Jesus' liberating power, those who do read the Bible may not understand what they read.

They are crying out—not always verbally but sometimes in negative behaviors—for the God-called preachers from the bushes as well as from the seminaries to come, sit with them, and to interpret the meaning of God amid their trying, tempting, tantalizing, and tormenting life struggles. They are often overwhelmed by fears and failures. Like Philip, the preacher of the African American tradition always had an interpretation and a proclamation, which brought succor and strength to enable a pilgrim people to live creatively and with dignity. The proclamation took the form of public declarations about the whole counsel of God, that is, the will and the way of God, which was preached with great conviction. Like a messenger fresh from before the throne of God, the preacher appeared before the congregation and proclaimed release for the captives. The proclamation was good news for the poor.

However, American history is spotted with incidents of the "cup running over" of those who were robbed of liberty and justice. Time and time again the objections to these injustices have been manifested in civil disobedience and even riots in our nation, a nation that advocates human rights around the world and does not ensure equal human rights for all citizens. Yet it has been the preaching—interpretation and proclamation of the gospel—that has kept hope alive in the African American community.

The Problem

This positive preaching tradition is being challenged by several factors. First, we are living in a period of rising secularism. James Earl Massey said:

> Our generation stands lost in a wilderness of secularity, relativism, proneness to question, and the loss of any felt need to be accountable. The judgment of sinful, selfish living

weighs heavily upon life in our time, and the evidences of a diseased human condition continue to suggest the need for help from beyond ourselves.[2]

The people to whom we preach today are stranded in the wilderness of secularism and relativism. The sin of greed and the struggle for power have been manifested in selfish living and have affected the entire nation. As always, those numbered among the least suffer the severest brunt of any malady. Only by a return to the God of our ancestors will we be able to restore meaning and dignity to the lives of this and future generations. But the return to the God of our ancestors can take place only among a generation that has a clear concept about God as deliverer and redeemer. The best way to introduce this idea of God to a people engulfed in secularism and relativism is to do so through the preaching tradition of the African American pastor-theologians.

A second aspect of the problem is urbanization and ghettoization, bringing to bear an additional negative effect upon a growing number of African Americans. Trapped in the urban centers of our nation with ever-diminishing resources for education, housing, health care, governmental services (police, fire protection, sanitation, and so on), and the concomitant burdens, we are experiencing an unprecedented rise in unemployment, use of illegal drugs, crime, and homelessness. Thus, we have ever-expanding ghettos across our nation. These problems are also rapidly spreading to the heretofore "safe" rural areas.

Over the last two decades, with the unprecedented rise in the drug culture, it seems that the church, through its preaching and practical theology, has lost some of its ability to shape the guiding principles, moral values, respect for righteousness, and sense of sacredness among the nonchurched. Children are being brought up in families without a male presence and where mothers and grandmothers are themselves nonchurched. There is no one to transmit religious values to these children. Along with urbanization and ghettoization come secularization and idolatry. The gods of drugs and the gods of violence are being enthroned all over America. How long can a people maintain their sanity in the face of an ever encroaching ghettoized and hopeless situation?

The interpretation and proclamation of the gospel from the African American traditional pulpits of the past provided hope for the victims. It also spoke with great force and fortitude to the sinful social structures and the perpetuators of an unjust social and economic system. It impelled the victims to rise up and to participate in God's plan for their redemption. It condemned sin and negative behaviors in the lives of individuals, but it also condemned the evil social structure that caused and allowed to exist conditions that preyed upon the dispossessed. This African American preaching tradition could provide some light in the dark and dismal situation in America today if the powers that be would take heed. They must take heed because the doom of the cities is the beginning of the doom of the nation. The African American preaching tradition will not only provide hope for the secularized and the ghettoized dispossessed of our nation, it will point out new directions for the transformation of an unjust socioeconomic system. The choices are clear. There must be a positive response by the victims and the victimizers to correct the injustices or they will succumb to the inevitable explosion of the time bomb set by the socioeconomic system of greed and exploitation in America.

Third, there is a neofundamental movement in our country that has made inroads into the African American religious community. The practitioners of this movement are preoccupied with the inerrancy of Scripture, personal salvation, and the like. "But few of their interpretations," as Howard Thurman pointed out, "deal with what the teachings and the life of Jesus have to say to those who stand, at a moment in human history, with their backs against the wall."

The need for profound belief in God and personal salvation are the important issues in Christianity; however, the methodology for achieving those objectives should be modeled on the method of Jesus himself. Jesus encountered persons at the point of their need. J. Deotis Roberts, a senior black theologian and author, put it this way:

> We must in no way abandon an intense concern for personal sin and salvation. We are becoming aware, however, that sinful social structures often destroy persons, families, and communities.[3]

The demand for social justice resounded in the traditional African American sermons, and the hearers always understood the divine relationship between their wholeness and their holiness. Wholeness and holiness were never juxtaposed in dichotomous positions. In fact, wholeness and holiness were inextricably intertwined in historic African American preaching.

These several aspects of the problem may be summed up in words from the prophet Nehemiah, ". . . The city, the place of my fathers' sepulchres, *lieth* waste, and the gates thereof are consumed with fire" (Nehemiah 2:3, KJV). The plethora of problems affecting the African American community are being manifested in the devastation of traditional religious values, and this generation is being consumed with a kind of raging fire of frustration, hopelessness, and godlessness.

Two Suppositions

Two suppositions form the basis for this book. First, African American preaching has been and is today the primary medium for reaching and communicating religious truths and values to the masses of our people. Although Christian education programs are expanding in our churches around the nation, the preacher is still the mass communicator of spiritual and moral truths and values.

Second, while there may be a variety of preaching styles, the basic content of historical African American preaching is practical theology, a theology that reflects upon the mandate, mission, and ministries of the church.

I am convinced that a study, preservation, presentation, and application of the African American interpretation and proclamation tradition—practical theology and preaching—will enhance the sacred and the secular life of this and future generations. It will reaffirm for the dispossessed that God is concerned about their concrete struggles for parity. It will challenge those in power to make real the promises of liberty and justice for all.

With the revival and perpetuation of the African American preaching tradition, a secularized, urbanized, and ghettoized people might join with those of Isaiah's time and declare:

How beautiful upon the mountains
   are the feet of the messenger
   who announces peace,

who brings good news,
   who announces salvation,
who says to Zion, "Your God reigns."
          —Isaiah 52:7 (NRSV).

The prophets and preachers of old came with a word of assurance and a word of hope in seemingly hopeless conditions.

Focus of This Book

James Cone was correct when he said:

> Theology is not universal language about God. Rather, it is human speech informed by historical and theological traditions, and written for particular times and places. Theology is *contextual* language—that is, defined by the human situation that gives birth to it. No one can write theology for all times, places, and persons.[4]

Preaching is the telling of some aspect of the divine story in various contexts with conviction. Practical theology affirms and clarifies mission and ministries in the church and in the world.

Theologians and preachers make their statements in contextual settings, responding to questions and making assertions based on experiences in their particular times and places. Some contend that their theological claims are objective and are applicable irrespective of times, places, and experiences. Rebecca S. Chopp responded to such a fallacy this way:

> Feminist theologians . . . make clear that the experience most often reflected upon is that of white bourgeois males. Out of reflecting upon this experience . . . theologians arrive at an interpretation of what they call *common* human experience.[5]

They also imply that these interpretations are correct and superior to any other interpretation by any other group. To correct this matter, Chopp suggested that, in the theological enterprise, we can't just "add woman and stir." I contend that there must be a radical new approach in the theological methodology that begins with the indigenous, situational context and experience of each particular group. In the existing materials that are available on preaching and theology and on the theology of preaching, we can't just "add African Americans and stir." Therefore, this book will focus on preaching and practical theology specifically from the African American perspective.

I make no claim that African American practical theology has any superiority over any other interpretation on the matter of practical theology. Practical theology from the African American perspective, as from all other perspectives, is indigenous and contextual.

God is neither indigenous nor contextual; yet God has chosen to be revealed in different ways in indigenous and contextual settings around the world. God has chosen not to overwhelm the indigenous with the universal. Only God is universal; the only claim my group can make is that resulting from the small disclosure that God has made in our faithful community.

If any group had all of the universal truths about God, then it would have achieved the reality of the lie that Satan used to deceive Adam and Eve in the garden of Eden. When forbidden to eat of the tree in the center of the garden and told that if they violated that prohibition they would die, Satan said, "God knows that when you eat of it your eyes will be opened, and you will be like God . . ." (Genesis 3:5, NRSV). Any group that believes it has the whole truth is trying to be like God.

This study is important because no one can make a proper assessment of the value of African American theology and preaching based on the criteria established by any group of theologians and preachers outside of the African American faith community. The value of the African American preaching and theological traditions must be judged by the results of that preaching-theological tradition as manifested in that particular community rather than by the rules established by those from the other side of town.

A study and presentation of practical theology in preaching in the African American community today will raise the consciousness and sensitivity of those who preach in the African American churches to the need for the continuation of practical theology in their preaching. It will also reaffirm for those who hear this preaching that God is concerned about their life struggles and situations as well as their eternal salvation.

This study and presentation will help non-African Americans to understand and appreciate the practical theological preaching that has been a motivating and empowering force for African Americans. Practical theology is the avenue to realized redemption for African Americans as we go into the twenty-first century.

"The black preacher," said Henry H. Mitchell, "is not an army officer ordering men to their death. Rather he is a crucial witness declaring how men ought to *live*."[6] What is the theological orientation of this "black preacher" who proclaims with urgency and conviction how human beings ought to live? This is the focus of this book.

Preaching and Theology

To the African American community, preaching and theology have been opposite sides of the same coin. Theology is like a mother guiding her child in a swimming pool to keep the child from going off into the "deep end." Theology guides preaching in elucidating revealed, eternal, and transcendent truths without going off into the "deep end" of sectism and cultism.

Preaching's role in theology is similar to that of a father teaching one of his children how to drive a car in and through an urban downtown setting. Pedestrians and traffic impinge upon the driver, but this is the only route available to reach the destination. Preaching has been the primary vehicle of theology in the African American churches. And, in spite of all the social, political, and economic obstacles challenging the existence and progress of this people, preaching has been the primary vehicle for transmitting transcendent theological truths to the homes and hearts of the masses.

Educational centers and programs are in operation by African American churches and institutions across this nation, but I contend that even with these centers and programs, which were not so prevalent three decades ago, still the majority of the religionists in these communities get their theology from the preached Word rather than through the various Christian education ministries. This points to the awesome responsibility that rests upon the shoulders of the African American preachers. It also points to the need for study, discussion, and preservation of this important subject of theology and preaching. However, we must do everything possible to get the masses of the members of our churches involved in our Christian education programs. To depend on the preaching to carry out the theological mandate is no longer adequate or acceptable.

Today, preaching is still the primary vehicle of theology in the African American churches. When the Word of God is preached, the most important event in the life of the church and the lives of the people takes place. While it is true today that many of our congregants seem to be more celebrative during the singing period of our worship experience, the preaching is still the most sacred element of the liturgy.

Preaching has always been viewed as a sacred art. Gifted preachers, or those who could "tell the story" with conviction to the extent that the hearers were motivated to act on their convictions, were specially ordained and anointed by God to be creative and artistic in preaching. This artistic ability was of divine bestowal and was the means of communicating theological truths and concerns for their temporal conditions. Historical African American preachers did practice to improve their artistic preaching style. "Most of the best Black preaching," Mitchell said, "maintains depth and relevance by means of art rather than argument . . ."[7]

"Preaching" may be defined as the interpretation and proclamation of the "Good News," some aspect of the gospel, with a view toward persuasion, edification, education, and empowerment.

It is a divine undertaking. Gardner C. Taylor warned:

> Preaching is a presumptuous business. If the undertaking does not have some sanctions beyond human reckoning, then it is, indeed, rash and audacious for one person to dare to stand up before or among other people and declare that he or she brings from the Eternal God a message for those who listen which involves issues nothing less than those of life and death.[8]

Theology provides the content of our preaching. Theology is the conclusion that practitioners in a particular faith community draw from thinking and talking about the message and meaning of the Christian faith. Carl Braaten was correct when he stated:

> Theology has no higher calling than to make straight the way for preaching the gospel of Jesus Christ. It has been my intention . . . to make my theology and preaching keep an eye on each other. Neither should be up to something the other cannot understand or approve.[9]

Preaching is vehicle and theology is content. Beyond theology and preaching, we have also concerned ourselves with the theology of preaching.

A Theology of Preaching

A theology of preaching in African American thought is not to be equated with preaching theology. Yet this is not to say that we are not engaged in theological preaching. For example, we do engage in doctrinal, exegetical, and hermeneutical preaching.

A theology of preaching is the acknowledgment and affirmation that preaching is the primary, divine mandate and medium for communicating, elucidating, and illuminating God's revelation for God's people. A theology of preaching affirms the sacred authority of the preacher to preach the whole counsel of God— to interpret God's revelations in the Scriptures, in Jesus Christ, in the Holy Spirit, and in the living church, and to proclaim God's revelation about the world to come. Paul Tillich declared:

> A theological system is supposed to satisfy two basic needs: the statement of the truth of the Christian message and the interpretation of this truth for every new generation. Theology moves back and forth between two poles, the eternal truth of its foundation and the temporal situation in which the eternal truth must be received.[10]

The theology that has been explicit in African American preaching has never been abstract and esoterical. It has always responded to the questions raised in life circumstances. Like King Zedekiah, African Americans, in their plight, have continued to ask, "Is there *any* word from the Lord" (Jeremiah 37:17, KJV) that addresses our particular conditions, needs, and aspirations? Practical theology responds in the affirmative through the preached Word.

Practical theology is just one of the fields in Christian theology. It stands alongside foundational or historical theology—the study of past theological systems; philosophical theology—the use of philosophy to rethink the creed of a particular religion; biblical theology—the Bible being the center of the theological discourse; systematic theology—the systematic organization and discussion of the Christian faith; and so forth.

The tendency to give systematic theology some higher status on the theological totem pole is an error. In response to this, Tillich declared that exegesis and homiletics can be just as theological as systematics and that it is unfortunate that the name "theology" has been reserved for systematics, particularly when systematics may fail to be theological as well as the others.[11]

This book will examine theological statements and sermons that illustrate preaching and practical theology and will offer observations from my experience as a pastor-theologian. While there are several regions in practical theology, my study will be limited to preaching and practical theology from a selected number of sermons by African American preachers and from theological statements from a cross section of the religious community.

Many great African American preachers have made significant contributions to the preaching and practical theology tradition of the African American. There are many who are profound bearers of this tradition today. However, it is impossible to mention all of them in this limited study. Some readers, then, will not find the name of their premier preacher mentioned in this work. Those, deceased or living, who have been mentioned were arbitrarily selected from the published works, manuscripts, and audiotapes in the possession of this writer. This is not to suggest that these were or are the greatest preachers among us. We have had and we still have great preachers all over this nation. I am indebted to them all.

I believe that a survey of the history of literary theology—articles and books—by African American preachers, religious leaders, and scholars will be helpful to the readers, so this will be the focus of chapter 2.

Chapter 2

History and Promise
of Literary Black Theology

Black theology is a theology in the making and only the Lord of the Church knows at this moment the ultimate direction it will take (1973).[1]
Black theology has come of age. It is now a dialogue partner with theological developments around the world (1987).[2]

The Background

Literary black theology here means the advancement of large volumes of articles and the writing of books—the production of literature on the subject of theology and related topics. The discussion is important for two reasons. One, it provides a brief review for those who have been involved in the development or the study of black theology. Two, it provides a brief survey of the development of literary black theology for many younger pastors, preachers, and laypersons who were not active in the civil rights, Black Power or black theology movements and who have not had the opportunity to study black theology.

I believe that this brief reflection upon the development of black theology provides an essential background on preaching and practical theology, which is a new region of exploration for black theology.

The term "black" rather than "African American" will be used more extensively in this chapter to refer to people of African descent. It reflects the language in use during the historical period covered in this chapter.

Having made its grand entrance into the arena of literary

13

theology two and one-half decades ago, black theology has not only survived, it has triumphed in a hostile environment. This hostility, particularly from the majority Christian community, was manifested in a variety of ways: it was questioned as to its validity, ignored as irrelevant, condemned as heretical, rejected as radical and racist, and relegated to the parade of a passing fad.

It is ironic that the hostility toward black theology came from within the black community as well as from outside. Within the black church community, there were many pastors and preachers who had been trained or theologically cultured in literary Euro-American theology. They adopted the Euro-American literary theology as universal and normative. They had not realized that Euro-American theology was indigenous to, captured by, and reflective of the social class, culture, and tradition of white Euro-American males standing in the position of superiority, power, and authority.

On the other hand, the sermons and teachings of most of these black pastors and preachers reflected a theology that was an interpretation or a reinterpretation of the Christian gospel in the light of the social and oppressive condition of African Americans. They preached a black theology. The irony was that they accepted a literary Euro-American theology as normative while they preached a gospel of liberation not then found in Euro-American literary theology.

In light of the emerging "Black Power" movement of the 1960s, it was more the term "black theology" than the content of literary black theology that was troublesome for many black pastors and preachers. The term "Black Power" had come to be associated with inciting riots and physical violence, over and against the nonviolent movement that was being led by the late Dr. Martin Luther King Jr. Black theology did not support the idea of physical violence. Black theology meant the production of literature on theology beginning in the indigenous black community of faith.

Theology is the conclusion that we draw from analytical thinking and talking about the message and meaning of a religious faith by a person or persons within that particular faith community. Theology is the expression of the message and meaning of that particular religious faith in the clearest and most coherent language possible.

The emergence of black theology grew out of the awareness that doing literary theology for a particular faith community must be the undertaking of a practitioner of that particular faith community. Thus, literary black theology had to be undertaken by theologians, scholars, and pastors who shared in the black religious experience.

The early practitioners and advocates of black theology bore the double burden of first defending the new concept "black theology" and, second, spelling out its content. Early black theology had to be defensive and offensive; it had to be apologetic and eristic. It had to defend its position in the intellectual theological community and in the church community in general. It also had to take the offensive and become eristic by calling into dispute existing theological treatises that, by some, claimed to be normative and yet overlooked or outrightly denied the social-justice aspect of the Judeo-Christian gospel.

The validation of black theology, then, was also an internal matter. Black theology could not be validated or invalidated by the rules established by Euro-American theologians. Euro-American theology is theology from the top down—theology from the powerful. It is a theology worked out by the privileged class. Black theology is theology from the bottom up—theology from the powerless. Black theology is a reflection upon the meaning and message of the Christian faith in the community of the underprivileged and the oppressed.

Euro-American theology and black theology have been in conflict with each other, the majority group having a superior attitude, presenting its theology as normative while viewing the emerging theology of the minority group as somewhat primitive. This was the attitude held by Euro-American theologians and church persons two and one-half decades ago. Unfortunately, some still hold this biased view. But this is being worked out in dialogue among those who see themselves as partners with mutual respect for each other rather than unequal partners.

Black theology has had more than its share of criticism from without and from within. It has not only endured, but is now in dialogue with theological developments around the world.

Literary "black theology" is an extension of the oral theology that provided the content for "black" preaching in North America. Oral theology is the verbal declarations and interpretations of the Christian faith by black preachers and laypersons that were not heretofore put into writing on a large scale. This oral theology began to be expressed in literary form in the mid-1960s. By 1973, J. Deotis Roberts said that "black theology is a theology in the making." And, fourteen years later, he declared that "black theology has come of age."

Current literary black theology is now moving through its third stage. The first was the beginning stage. The second was the development stage, and now, third, is the international dialogue stage. Here we are talking about a black theology produced in writing.

The Beginning

The use of the term "Black Power" established a new watershed in the civil rights movement in America. Martin Luther King Jr. and others had been in the forefront of the civil rights movement for a decade, since 1955. Many persons had paid the ultimate sacrifice in their nonviolent attempt to bring about social change and to improve the deplorable condition of the inhumane treatment of black folk in America by the oppressive majority.

In 1966 this nation was experiencing its most sustained racial unrest and confrontations. The slogan "Black Power" resounded like a cannon around the nation on college and university campuses and in the ghettos of our metropolitan areas.

"The term 'Black Power' was first used in the civil rights movement in the spring of 1966 by Stokely Carmichael to designate the only appropriate response to white racism,"[3] said James Cone. The slogan "Black Power" meant different things to different people, from civil disobedience to the overthrow of the colonial, imperialistic, and oppressive system in America.

For some, it meant "black people taking the dominant role in determining the black-white relationship in American society."[4] For others, it meant "complete emancipation of black people from white oppression by whatever means black people deem necessary."[5]

By 1967 Stokely Carmichael and Charles V. Hamilton had coauthored the book *Black Power: The Politics of Liberation in America*.[6] In 1968 the Reverend Albert B. Cleage Jr. published

The Black Messiah: The Religious Roots of Black Power.[7] Carmichael and Hamilton contended that their book was about "why, where and in what manner black people in America must get themselves together. It is about black people taking care of business—the business of and for black people." Failure in this effort, they contended, would leave black people in subjection to those who were unwilling to give up power, position, and authority. Success would mean "we will exercise control over our lives politically, economically and physically."[8]

Speaking of the civil rights movement and the Black Power revolution of the 1960s, Cleage said that "Jesus was a revolutionary black leader, a Zealot, seeking to lead a Black Nation to freedom, so the Black Church must carefully define the nature of the revolution."[9] Here he was indirectly calling for a theological interpretation of the revolution in light of the black church's understanding of the mission, ministry, and teachings of Jesus Christ.

The book was a volume of sermons preached to black people. It was published in the hope, said Cleage, of helping black people find their way back to the black Messiah. It was also published in response to the request of many black preachers who were attempting to "make their preaching relevant to the complex and urgent needs of the black community." White people who might read the book, he noted, were "permitted to listen to a black man talking to black people."[10]

Many articles and several other books were written on the subject of Black Power, black religion, and the black experience as we moved through the 1960s. The two mentioned above—one from outside the church, *Black Power*, and one from inside the church, *The Black Messiah*—are not suggested to be the best models of the literature from that period, but they are normative and reflect well the tone and tenor of the leaders from outside and from inside the church at that time.

"Black Power" became such a powerful term that it sent black folk running into the streets—again, particularly the students on the college and university campuses and the folk in the ghettos around the nation—to take matters into their own hands in an attempt to throw off the yoke of segregation, humiliation, and exploitation in America. They felt that the oppressors in this nation were irresponsive to the nonviolent civil rights movement over the previous decade.

"Black Power" became the slogan that sent white folk running for shelter from the impending and actual riots that
erupted across America. They sought shelter through paternal-
istic relationships with submissive black leaders. They sought
shelter behind the extensive and brutal use of repressive police
power against both the rioters and the nonviolent protesters.
Eventually they sought shelter by turning to the progressive
black religious leaders of the nation.

Through the white press, these power brokers asked the
African American preachers, who were the natural community
leaders and church theologians, what they had to say about the
erupting "Black Power movement." They expected these progressive African American church leaders to come out with a
condemnation. However, to their surprise as well as that of
those in the African American religious community, these leaders came out with a theological interpretation of the new and
threatening concept, "Black Power." Their response set in mo-
tion a new movement in literature in black theology.

Forty-seven clergymen and one female layperson, Dr. Anna
Arnold Hedgemen—the Commission on Religion and Race of
the National Council of Churches in New York—met and
drafted the first theological statement, which appeared in the
New York Times on July 31, 1966. The statement opened:

> We, an informal group of Negro churchmen in America,
> are deeply disturbed about the crisis brought upon our coun-
> try by historic distortions of important human realities in the
> controversy about "black power." What we see shining
> through the variety of rhetoric is not anything new but the
> same old problem of power and race which has faced our
> beloved country since 1619.[11]

They further stated their realization that neither the term
"power" nor the term "Christian conscience" were easy terms
to discuss, especially in the context of race relations then existing in America. There was a fundamental distortion in the
controversy about "Black Power," they noted. This distortion
was "rooted in the gross imbalance of power and conscience
between Negroes and white Americans." The problem was the
confrontation between conscienceless power and powerless

conscience. They continued:

> The power of white men is corrupted because it meets little meaningful resistance from Negroes to temper it and keep white men from aping God. The conscience of black men is corrupted because, having no power to implement the demands of conscience, the concern for justice is transmuted into a distorted form of love, which, in the absence of justice, becomes chaotic self-surrender.[12]

This was a powerful theological statement on the concept of "Black Power." It set the stage for the future of an African American literary theological treatise. This was a practical theological statement that indicated there ought to be a mutual relationship between human conscience and human power. Human conscience and human power ought to complement each other. But in the actual life situation of the people, the dominant group held the power and wielded it without conscience, while the dominated group was very conscious of the human condition and the human aspiration of the poor, but had no power to implement a positive program of redemption. So the reality of Christian love in action had been distorted, and social justice for the downtrodden continued to be an illusion.

This group became the National Committee of Negro Churchmen (NCNC). In further interpreting the signs of the time, its members refused to blame the victims; so, in a statement about the riots, they said: "These events, we believe, are but the expression of the judgment of God upon our nation for its failure to use its abundant resources to serve the real well-being of people, at home and abroad."[13] Ultimate power, they said, belonged to God alone.

This idea of God's judgment and God's power was a clear reflection of the theological content of this statement and of their weekly sermons. The NCNC statement was entitled "Black Power," and it was divided into four points likened to the three- and four-point sermons they preached weekly before their congregations.[14]

The first division of the statement was addressed "To the Leaders of America: Power and Freedom." Here they announced full support for the civil rights movement and its leaders. They pointed out that the greatest threat to our nation was not the riots in our big cities, nor the disagreement among leaders of the civil rights movement, nor the cries of "Black Power." The threat to the nation was the misusing and abusing of American power. They deplored the overt violence of the riots, but added, "We believe it is more important to focus on the real sources of the eruptions." In summary, they declared that "when American leaders are forced by the American people to quit misusing and abusing American power, then will the cry for 'black power' become inaudible."

The second part was addressed "To White Churchmen: Power and Love." Here they pointed out that the controlling element in power should be love and not the power itself. They warned that as long as white churchmen would continue to moralize and to misinterpret the true meaning of Christian love, justice would also continue to be subverted in the land.

The third point was addressed "To Negro Citizens: Power and Justice." In this section they called the Negroes to an under-standing of the need for collective power and organizational power rather than power and opportunity for selected indi-viduals. They pointed out the need for reconciliation of the Negroes among themselves and an improved self-image, which brings a sense of pride. Then they called on the churches to use more of their resources in working for human justice.

The fourth and final statement was addressed "To the Mass Media: Power and Truth." They praised the mass media for doing a commendable job during the Southern demonstrations, even to the extent that, though many of them were mauled and injured, they still stuck to the task, making clear to the eyes and ears of the world "the ugly truth of the brutalizing system of overt discrimination and segregation." In 1966 they said the task would be more difficult because the truth that needed revealing was not as clear-cut as it was in the segregated South. Thus, the media would have to look to a variety of sources. And just as the media did not rely on police records and establishment figures to present the brutalizing truth about Mississippi, they would now have to operate in that same fashion in New York, Cleveland, and Chicago.

They offered any help that they could render and said the fate of the country, to no small extent, depended upon the truth that they would disclose.

This was a theology of "Black Power." It was a practical theology formulated first, not by academic theologians, but by pastor-theologians. In summary, this theology of "Black Power" affirmed that only God had ultimate power, and that America's leadership was misusing its power in relationship to black Americans. The NCNC asserted that the judgment of God, meaning the wrath of God, was set against the nation, and the riots were a manifestation of God's displeasure.

This was the beginning of literary "black" or African American theology. Note well that in its beginning stage the laborers were primarily African American clergy members. For the next four years a succession of other theological statements were issued by the NCNC, other clergy members, and other African American church persons and scholars. It was the clergy members who were to return to their congregations and clarify the signs of the time and their theological meaning through the interpretation and proclamation of the gospel to the people. The sermons of Albert Cleage are representative of the preaching of that era. So, the first African American literary theology was church theology dealing with the practical issues in the life situation of the people.

In the meantime, black theologians and scholars were developing a literature in black theology. James Cone rocked the established theological boat with his explosive book *Black Theology and Black Power* in 1969. Of the concept of "Black Power," Cone said:

> If, as I believe, Black Power is the most important development in American life in this century, there is a need to begin to analyze it from a theological perspective. In this work an effort is made to investigate the concept of Black Power, placing primary emphasis on its relationship to Christianity, the Church, and contemporary American theology.[15]

James Cone was insisting through the power of the pen and the insights of the black church that the term "Black Power" had theological significance. This idea was consistent with the declaration of the pastor-theologians of the NCNC. This marked the beginning of modern radicalism in black academic theology.

Earlier literary expressions of black theology, although they were not labeled as such, would include the writings of Howard

Thurman and the late educator, college administrator, and theologian Benjamin E. Mays.

In 1949 Thurman published *Jesus and the Disinherited*.[16] This book gave a radical view of the mission, ministry, and teachings of Jesus, as compared with the general view in the majority culture. Throughout, Thurman showed that Jesus' ministry in the world addressed the needs and aspirations of the disinherited. He pointed out that the concern of Jesus was still for the disinherited, which happened to be the Negroes in America of his day.

Benjamin E. Mays published *The Negro's God as Reflected in His Literature* in 1938.[17] He said his aim was "to tell America what the Negro thinks of God."[18] Mays publication included a collection of excerpts from sermons, prayers, spirituals, poems, and essays covering the period of 1760 to 1937. The readers would discover that these excerpts espoused a theology that was just as "radical" as that espoused in the sermons of Cleage or the *Black Theology and Black Power* of James Cone. Mays included a quotation from Kelly Miller that was a radical statement about the misuse and abuse of white power:

> Power may seem to triumph for a while; might may be enthroned while right is enchained; but final defeat is never accepted until the verdict is reversed, and right is crowned victor.[19]

What appeared to be a new rise of radical literature in black theology being advanced by Cone and others was merely the literary articulation of a black theological oral tradition. They were now saying through the print media what was being said only vocally, primarily from the pulpits, in the past.

Cone's second book, *A Black Theology of Liberation*, was published in 1970.[20] Then, in 1971 J. Deotis Roberts published *Liberation and Reconciliation: A Black Theology*.[21]

By the early 1970s, black caucuses had formed in virtually every major white denomination with a black constituency. These caucuses served at least three major functions. One, they were the interpreters of the new concepts "Black Power" and "black theology" in these denominations. Two, they sensitized these denominations to their own practice and sanction of overt and covert racism. And, three, they implored their denominations to use their influence and resources to dislodge racism and oppression in America and colonialism and oppression around the world.

The ministers in these caucuses also preached regularly a gospel of redemption—liberation and confederation—to their people Sunday after Sunday. Their preaching inspired and empowered their people to survive, to endure, to struggle and overcome.

By this time, African American theology was sanctioned and rapidly spreading in the academic arena. Cone and Roberts were the leading African American academic theologians. There were other significant contributors to the early movement, including Gayraud S. Wilmore, C. Eric Lincoln, Henry Mitchell, and Major Jones. Of course, this does not exhaust the extended list of major contributors to the black theology enterprise.

Although both Cone and Roberts called for greater cooperation between the academic theologians and the church—preacher-theologians—we have not made significant advancement in this matter.

There have been sporadic meetings between pastor-theologians and academic theologians over the years. However, the first national dialogue among African American church leaders and theologians was held October 19-21, 1992. (I will say more about this event later.)

The first stage of African American literary theology was its formation, generally from 1966 through 1976. By this time the great battle of apologetics—reasoned defense (and many times angry defense) of the term "black theology"—was not over. But, by 1976, several European theologians and several white American theologians were forced, by overwhelming evidence, to recognize the legitimacy of the development of a theology from the experience, meaning, and message of the Christian faith among people in America of African descent.

One of the European theologians giving special attention to black theology during its early period of development was Helmut Gullwitzer, professor of systematic theology with the faculty in philosophy at the Free University in Berlin. He wrote an article in 1975 titled "Why Black Theology?" In it, he made the following assertion about white theologians with reference to the emergence of black theology:

The naiveté in which the theologian has hitherto accepted theological thought and the context of the tradition in which it takes place—as universally addressed to all men, valid, accessible, and useful for all men in the same way—breaks to pieces. He suddenly sees himself together with the world to which he belongs from the outside, as it were, from the perspective of another community and another historical fate.[22]

Here Gullwitzer acknowledged that black theology was beneficial in expanding the heretofore existing theological system.

Other European theologians responding positively to the emerging black theology during this period included Jürgen Moltmann, Henry Mottu, Bruno Chenu, and George Casalis.[23]

One white American theologian addressing the matter of black theology by 1976 was Paul L. Lehmann, the Charles Briggs professor emeritus of systematic theology of Union Theological Seminary in New York. The black theology of James H. Cone, he said, ". . . rightly brought me up short on the omission of specific attention to black Americans in *Ethics in a Christian Context*."[24] Lehmann recognized that black theology had shown him that he had omitted the thoughts of black Americans in his works on theology and ethics.

Other white American theologians who engaged in the discussion of black theology in a positive way by 1976 included Peter C. Hodgson, Frederick Herzog, Benjamin Reist, G. Clarke Chapman Jr., Glenn R. Bucher, Rosemary Ruether, and John Carey.[25]

The great dispute over the meaning of love and justice and liberation in Christian theology raged on, but with the concomitant emergence of Latin American liberation theology, European political theology, feminist theology, and the birth of African and Asian theologies, black theology had the opportunity to move from formation to further development.

The Development

The stages of the development of black theology do overlap. But generally from the mid-1970s to the early 1980s it went through its second stage—a swift period of maturation. By then it had been well established as a black theology of liberation. In

1969, the NCNC—the pastor-theologians—declared:

> Black Theology is a theology of black liberation. It seeks to plumb the black condition in the light of God's revelation in Jesus Christ, so that the black community can see that the gospel is commensurate with the achievement of black humanity. Black Theology is a theology of "blackness." It is the affirmation of black humanity that emancipates black people from white racism. . . . The message of liberation is the revelation of God as revealed in the incarnation of Jesus Christ. Freedom IS the gospel. Jesus is the Liberator![26]

From the black academic community, Cone made the following assertion in 1970:

> Black Theology is a theology of liberation because it is a theology which arises from an identification with the oppressed blacks of America, seeking to interpret the gospel of Christ in the light of the black condition. It believes that the liberation of black people *is* God's liberation.[27]

And Roberts said in 1971:

> Freedom sums up *what is*. Liberation is revolutionary—for blacks it points to *what ought to be*. Black Christians desire radical and rapid social change in America as a matter of survival. Black Theology is a theology of *liberation*."[28]

Black theology could move through its developmental stage for several reasons. First, it had clearly established its core motif as liberation theology both through the pastor-theologians and through the academic theologians during the formative period. Black liberation theology in North America could be distinguished from other theologies, such as liberation theology in Latin America, Asian liberation theology, and African theology. While all of these theologies had liberation as a core motif, they emerged out of different sociopolitical and economic backgrounds. For example, black liberation theology emerged out of a background of racism in America; for Latin America the problem was classism; in Africa and Asia the root problem was culturalism; in North America feminist theology was based on sexism; and Euro-American liberation theology was political theology.

The tide of black liberation theology could not be reversed because of the rising flood of similar liberation theologies around the world. Black liberation theology, thus, had a chance to develop and to mature from the mid-1970s to the early 1980s alongside other liberation theologies.

Second, black liberation theology was getting a favorable review by several European and North American white theologians.

Third, more African American pastor-theologians understood and accepted the term "black theology" and were using the term in their preaching and teaching. The members of the mass black churches were affirming black theology. Articles and books on the subject abounded. Major religious periodicals and journals carried articles on the topic.

Fourth and most important was the broadening of the scope of exploration of theological concepts in black theology. Roberts said of black theology in 1973:

> We need unity without uniformity to enable each Black scholar to do what he can do best. We need serious but creative scholarship. Some will be interested in a biblical theology; others will major in the historical or the philosophical approaches. Some will major in methodology, others in content. We will have our Bultmanns, Tillichs, Niebuhrs, and Barths. The problem of Black suffering will challenge some. The nature and mission of the Church will urge others on, while still others will pursue the Black messiah. . . . "The harvest is plentiful, but the laborers are few; pray therefore the Lord of the harvest to send out laborers into his harvest" (Luke 10:2, RSV).[29]

In fulfillment of this hope, by 1980 Roberts expanded his own black theology of liberation to include a discussion on family and church from a black theological perspective.[30] In his book *For My People: Black Theology and the Black Church*, Cone expanded the black liberation theme to focus on others, such as black theology and the black church, black theology and black women, the Third World, and other minorities.[31]

My own book, *Redemption in Black Theology*, attempted to move beyond the liberation motif in black theology and to advance a redemption theme from its Old Testament metaphorical usage, which included liberation and confederation.[32] The liberation aspect of redemption meant deliverance from oppression and Egyptian bondage, but it also meant the journey into and the formation of a new community in the land of Canaan. Black theology had moved from an enterprise designed to interpret the term "Black Power" and liberation to the discussion of church, family, women in the black church, and other theological concepts, such as redemption.

A fifth indication of the maturation of black theology was the rise of scholars from other academic disciplines joining it in addressing the matters of Black Power, black religion, and black experience in articles and books. One example was the book *Prophesy Deliverance! An Afro-American Revolutionary Christianity* by Cornel West. In this volume, West showed how "American philosophy has never taken the Afro-American experience seriously."[33] He attempted to correct this omission by addressing the subject of the black religious experience in America from the discipline of philosophy.

Others who addressed the subject of black religion in writing during this period included C. Eric Lincoln, who, as a sociologist of religion, wrote *The Black Church Since Frazier.*[34] Wyatt Tee Walker reviewed the black experience in music in his book *"Somebody's Calling My Name": Black Sacred Music and Social Change.*[35] Pastor-theologian Harold A. Carter wrote *The Prayer Tradition of Black People.*[36] From the discipline of religious education, James D. Tyms wrote *Spiritual (Religious) Values in the Black Poet.*[37] Historian Vincent Harding wrote *There Is a River: The Black Struggle for Freedom in America.*[38] These are just a few selected samples of the writings of these scholars on the subject of black religion from various academic disciplines.

With other disciplines focusing on black religion, and the black experience in general, black theology had the opportunity to mature as it clarified its own hypothesis, laid out its own presupposition, and interpreted its own theological meaning and tenants.

During the developmental period, 1976-1981, black theology became a respectable entity in the theological enterprise. It defined its own methodology—a theology from the bottom up and not the other way around. It certified itself as a practical theology with its foundation in the church, with its genesis in the pastor-theologians and now certified by the black academic theologians.

It matured through its critique of Euro-American theology, which overlooked or denied the black religious experience and faith in its theological enterprise. Black theology had intellectual forums in the lecture halls and in the printed pages all over this nation and it effectively established itself as a black theology of liberation. It also expanded its horizon beyond the interpretation of Black Power and liberation to include a broader spectrum of doctrines and biblical mandates. Black theology had come of age.

The International Dialogue

By the early 1980s black theology had made its mark in Europe, Africa, Asia, Latin America, and in the Caribbean. As Roberts wrote, it had become "a dialogue partner with theological developments around the world." In his book *Black Theology in Dialogue*, Roberts examined "Afro-American/African theological dialogue." He pointed out that one of the most difficult assignments of the Christian theologians, with interest in worldwide religions and theology, was to find a framework for discussion. Yet he found some common ground for dialogue with African theologians, namely, the Bible, tradition, theism, community, and Christology.[39] So, in spite of the difficulty in finding frameworks for dialogue with theologians of other cultures around the world, it was possible, and today African American theology is so engaged.

Then Roberts showed how black theology was in dialogue with Minjung theology, which was developing in South Korea. Minjung theology was cultural and historical but essentially political, he said, and he showed the lines along which a fruitful dialogue could take place between it and black theology. For example, there were similarities in both history and culture where the two theologies could inform each other.

Next he showed the relationship between Jewish liberation theology and black theology, but pointed out that the greatest affinity between them would be the faith that had "enabled both communities to translate the memory of suffering into a vessel of hope."[40] (The Old Testament stories of God's promises, protection, and deliverance have greatly influenced the theology and preaching in the African American churches.) Our brief period of theological maturation in the latter half of the 1970s to the early 1980s also saw the beginning of the third stage, that is, the dialogue with other theologies around the world.

Through this process, African American theology came of age through the 1980s. However, Roberts warned: "It is clear that the task of doing black theology lies more in the future than the past."[41]

In 1984 Roberts established the Foundation for Religious and Educational Exchange. This is a nonprofit organization that promotes cross-cultural, academic and grassroots, national and international, ecumenical and interreligious dialogue among scholars, students, and peoples around the world. It has awarded scholarships, directed seminars in Central America, conducted workshops, and plotted strategies for social change.

I was privileged to be among seventeen African American scholars, students, and church persons to travel to Buenos Aires and Argentina to participate in a cross-cultural and international, interreligious dialogue on a comparison between Latin American liberation theology and black theology, July 27 to August 7, 1992. The dialogue was held among participants from Germany, Switzerland, and Latin America, and included scholars, students, church leaders, and laypersons.

The first formal dialogue between African American theologians and African theologians took place in Dar es Salaam, Tanzania, August 22-28, 1971. The two primary themes of the dialogue were "Liberation" and "Africanization." African American theologians were focusing on politics and African theologians were focusing on culture, with neither denying the importance of the other. This enabled them "to learn from each other's experiences of oppression."[42]

As early as 1976, the Ecumenical Association of Third World Theologians (EATWOT) was formulated to promote dialogue among Third World theologians. The first EATWOT conference was held in Accra, Ghana, in December 1977 and focused on the future development of African theology.[43]

At the Asian Theological Conference (ATC) held in Wennappuwa, Sri Lanka, January 7-20, 1979, the nearly seventy-five Asian delegates included Protestants and Roman Catholics, with the Catholics in the majority. Fraternal delegates included representatives from Africa, Latin America, the Caribbean, and the United States.[44]

The delegates from the eleven Asian countries that made up the ATC were in search of an Asian theology that had its origin in the recognition that Euro-American theology was totally inadequate as a creative response to Asian reality. The theme of the ATC was "Asia's Struggle for Full Humanity: Toward a Relevant Theology."

Several conferences have been sponsored in various countries by EATWOT since that time, with African American theologians participating in the dialogue.[45]

Roberts's discussion on the African American dialogue with Minjung theology and Jewish theology are other examples of black theology in dialogue with other theologies around the world.

The seventy-third annual convocation at the Howard University School of Divinity (my alma mater) was held November 8-9, 1989. Its theme was "Black Theology in Retrospect and Prospect: Discontent, Revolt, and New Ferment." The focus was the fortieth anniversary of Thurman's *Jesus and the Disinherited* and the twentieth anniversary of Cone's *Black Theology and Black Power*.

Participants in that convocation included Cone, who was honored, Delores Carpenter, Luther Smith, Evans Crawford, Mozella Mitchell, Gayraud Wilmore, Deloris Williams, J. Deotis Roberts, Cain Hope Felder, Cornel West, Jacquelyn Grants, Dennis W. Wiley, Josiah Young, Lawrence N. Jones, James Forbes, and C. Eric Lincoln. All of these persons were major practitioners or contributors to black theology.

Concurrent with that convocation was the publication of *A Black Theology of Liberation: Twentieth Anniversary Edition*, with critical reflections by Gayraud Wilmore, Delores Williams, Rosemary Ruether, Pablo Richard, Robert McAfee Brown, and K. D. Abraham.[46] This was international dialogue. (Pablo Richard is Chilean and K. C. Abraham is vice president of EATWOT and professor of theology and ethics in Bangalore, India.) The foreword to the 1986 edition was taken from *The Politics of Education* by a Brazilian in exile, Paulo Freire. The dialogue in the book was interracial (Brown), intergenerational (Wilmore), intergender (Ruether and Williams) and international (Freire, Abraham, and Richard), which affirmed black theology's maturity and global partnerships.

On October 19-21, 1992, the first National Dialogue Conference on "What It Means to Be Black and Christian" was sponsored by the Kelly Miller Smith Institute on African American Church Studies at the Vanderbilt Divinity School in Nashville, Tennessee. More than two hundred African American theologians, scholars, pastors, students, and laypersons were in attendance. A few whites were also among us. About twenty-five presenters addressed various aspects of the subject.

Black theology has a rich and rewarding history. It is not only in dialogue with other theologies around the world, it is also expanding its dialogue between the church leaders and the academic community at home. In his preface and afterword to the twentieth anniversary edition of *A Black Theology of Liberation*, Cone made us keenly aware of our gender insensitivity in our early works in black theology. He also pointed out the need for the inclusion of global, economic, and class analysis of oppression in black theology. So we can see clearly with Roberts that our task "lies more in the future than in the past."[47] However, we do now have a rich foundation of literary black theology upon which we must continue to build. This is one objective of this book.

The Promise of Black Theology

As we move through the 1990s, African American theology has great promise. Some African American theologians will expand the dialogue with other theologies around the world; some will expand the national dialogue; others will major in womanist theology (and I hope that this project will not be left to female scholars alone; I also hope that all female scholars will not limit their research and contributions to womanist theology only); others will be preoccupied with global issues; and still others will explore other fields and regions in theology. The concept of redemption as *liberation* and *confederation* must be developed.

My current research is in the field of practical theology, focusing on the region of African American preaching and practical theology. This research has taken me back to the church theologians—the pastor-preacher-theologians—the place of the

beginning of literary "black theology." One objective is that of
bridging the gap rather than widening the chasm between
church theology and academic theology, that is, the ecclesia and
the academia. In this vast arena of theology, we cannot afford to
have "either/or," but we must develop "both/and" church
theology, that is, a practical theology among the masses of our
people, and an academic theology, that is, a theology among the
African American, Christian scholars. We have affirmed that
African American theology is still transmitted to the masses
through the preacher-theologians.

The entire global, plural, and ecumenical theological enterprise will be enriched as African American theological development and dialogue expand.

I hope that this brief survey of the beginning, the development, and the current dialogue state of black theology will help
the reader to appreciate my attempt to expand the enterprise of
black theology in my discussion of preaching and practical
theology from an African American perspective. I shall now
proceed to examine and discuss practical theology and practical
preaching as they have been manifested in the African American religious tradition.

Chapter 3

Practical Theology and Practical Preaching

I think we ought to just tell the story. And one of the things that older preachers did, they could tell the Bible story. And many of our great churches were built up, not on theology really, and we need theology, of course, but they were built up largely on preachers that could tell the Bible story.[1]

Affirming the Practical

The statement above from the late Reverend Dr. Sandy F. Ray, a nationally renowned African American Baptist preacher, is a telling testimony. It attests to the fact that African American churches and African American denominations have a tradition of humble birth and grandiose development with a practical theology communicated through the practical preaching of ministers who simply told the Bible story.

Ray not only affirmed the importance of storytelling in African American preaching, his preaching was *par excellence* in story preaching. He was, for many African American preachers, a model mentor. His preaching provided the stimulus for my master of divinity dissertation, titled "Black Preaching: The Style and Design of Dr. Sandy F. Ray."[2] We shall return to the discussion of storytelling in African American preaching later in this chapter.

Practical Theology

As stated in chapter 1, practical theology is just one of the fields in Christian theology. Although, historically and contem-

porarily, systematic theology is elevated as the norm for all
fields of theology, there have always been those who have held
different views on this matter. For example, Friedreich Schleiermacher praised practical theology as the crown of theology. For
Schleiermacher, practical theology was not a third part of theology in addition to historical and systematic theology but rather
the technical theory through which the other two parts, the
historical and the systematic, were to be applied in the life of the
church.[3]

Practical theology reflects upon the divine mandate for ministries through the church. It examines both the biblical mandate
and the present human condition and attempts to correlate the
two, giving divine sanction to the mission and ministries of the
church in every current world situation.

Practical theology in the African American perspective does
not study the history of the meaning of God as understood by
the church down through the years. This is the task of historical
theology. Practical theology does not attempt to explain the
attributes of God in technical, theological, and theoretical terms.
This is the task of systematic theology. However, practical theology, as revealed in African American preaching, affirms the
God of history. Practical theology also affirms the attributes of
God. In history, God is the One who, according to his own plan
of redemption, redeemed the Israelites from Egyptian bondage.
God is the One who redeemed the Hebrew children from the
fiery furnace. Thus, God is the One who has ordained a plan of
redemption and is in the process of redeeming the dispossessed
from human-caused suffering now.

God's attributes are summed up in the oral folk sermons—
not in puzzling, esoterical, or mystical terms, such as "omnipo-
tent," "omniscient," and "omnipresent," but as "so high, you
can't get over him, so wide you can't get around him, and so
low that you can't get under him." This practical theology is a
theology of *affirmation* rather than a theology of *explanation*. This
practical theology provides biblical and divine answers to the
questions implied or raised by those living on the underside of
an unjust society. It also provides the bridge between the eternal
Christian message of hope and the human situation, both generally and specifically. It gives directions for the church to be
involved in ministries in the world.

In African American religion practical theology is not a theory that was pondered in the theological laboratory and then presented and tested in the factories of real-life situations. Practical theology is a theology put together on the assembly line of existence in the experience of a pilgrim people. Its genesis, its beginning and development, was in orthopraxis rather than in orthodoxy. Orthodoxy is concerned with right beliefs and right doctrines, while orthopraxis is concerned with right action and right involvement in God's plan of redemption. Practical theology is concerned with right practice in human situations as revealed in the Word of God, in addition to right doctrine or theory about the will of God.

I am not suggesting that there was any conscious attempt on the part of African American church persons and theologians to initiate and to develop a practical theology. Like African American theology in general, practical theology is the product of the biblically based preaching and teaching of a people whose backs were and still are against the wall. When the oppressors were free to deliberate and to engage in debate about who God was in the world, the oppressed were forced by circumstances to construct a theological answer to what God was doing in the world—in the real world of their present and continuing plight.

For African Americans, the idea of social justice, human dignity, self-respect, and redemption as God-ordained birthrights did not emerge in the proverbial theological "ivory towers." It surfaced and developed among the people as they journeyed through the jungle of inhumanity in America. For example, Dr. Martin Luther King Jr. was exposed to the great thinkers on civil rights and human justice in Morehouse College in Atlanta and to the great theological minds in Crozer and Boston Theological Seminaries. However, when King spoke for himself about the shaping of his ideas, he drew upon the teachings of his family and his community during his developing years. His training in the graduate schools helped him to articulate his theology, but his foundational theological premises came from his church and family tradition. King told of his upbringing:

> As far back as I could remember, I had resented segregation, and had asked my parents questions about it. . . . My mother took me on her lap and began by telling me about

slavery and how it had ended with the Civil War. . . . Then she said the words that almost every Negro hears before he can yet understand the injustice that makes them necessary: "You are as good as anyone." I remember a trip to a downtown shoestore with Father when I was still small. We had sat down in the first empty seats at the front of the store. A young white clerk came up and murmured politely: "I'll be happy to wait on you if you'll just move to those seats in the rear."

My father answered, "There's nothing wrong with these seats. We're quite comfortable here."

"Sorry," said the clerk, "but you'll have to move."

"We'll either buy shoes sitting here," my father retorted, "or we won't buy shoes at all." Then he took me by the hand and walked out of the store. This was the first time I had ever seen my father so angry. I still remember walking down the street beside him as he muttered, "I don't care how long I have to live with this system, I will never accept it."[4]

Those experiences shaped the practical theological thinking and preaching of King in particular, and those experiences shaped the practical theological preaching in the African American churches in general. A practical theology of redemption provided the theological foundation for practical preaching, and practical preaching transmitted and perpetuated those practical, theological truths of redemption to the heads and hearts of the hearers.

Redemption for African Americans meant salvation from states and circumstances as well as salvation from sin, guilt, and the consequence thereof. Redemption meant liberation from oppression, and it also meant confederation, or the developing of a community of God.[5]

Practical Preaching

"Transformed nonconformist" is the title of one of the sermons in King's book *Strength to Love*.[6] The biblical text was: "Be not conformed to this world: but be ye transformed by the renewing of your mind . . ." (Romans 12:2, KJV). In this practical sermon, the preacher challenged the listeners to live as nonconformists to the social system of injustice. He preached:

"DO NOT CONFORM" is difficult advice in a generation when crowd pressures have unconsciously conditioned our minds and feet to move to the rhythmic drumbeat of the status quo. Many voices and forces urge us to choose the path of least resistance, and bid us never to fight for an unpopular cause and never to be found in a pathetic minority of two or three.[7]

King continued by noting that certain intellectual disciplines would persuade them to conform to get along and that, in the modern world, "everyone seems to crave the anesthetizing security of being identified with the majority."[8] But, in the face of all of these pressures and tendencies to conform, as Christians, he declared, we have the mandate to be nonconformists.

This was a practical sermon since it did not address some esoterical and cognitive idea of what it meant to be Christian. Rather, it addressed the listeners where they were amid all the complexities of injustice. It pointed out that to be Christians, really Christians, means to be nonconformists to the ideologies of the majority, even when it means fighting for the unpopular causes of the minority numbering as little as two or three. He declared that the cause of freedom is the Christian calling.

King was influenced by his family and his church. He was inspired by Walter Rauschenbush's *Christianity and the Social Crisis*. He was indelibly impressed by the teachings of Mahatma Gandhi:

> ... I came to see for the first time that the Christian doctrine of love, operating through the Gandhian method of nonviolence, is one of the most potent weapons available to an oppressed people in their struggle for freedom.[9]

Thus, though his practical theology focused on concerns for the oppressed, he engaged in practical preaching that inspired and impelled people from all walks of life—the rich, the poor, the educated, the illiterate, Catholics, Protestants, and Jews—to engage in the greatest nonviolent protest movement in the history of this nation. Remember, however, that the preaching of King was just one of the high-water marks in the preaching tradition of the African American churches. The multitudes that acted on the challenges in his preaching attracted international media attention and their voices resounded around the world.

His theological conviction was that, to strive toward social justice, even if it led to making the ultimate sacrifice, is a

Christian mandate. It led to the sermonic speech that he delivered in the Ebenezer Baptist Church in February 1968 titled
"Then My Living Will Not Be in Vain." In it he talked about the
day when he would become victimized by that common de-
nominator we call death. At his funeral, he maintained, he
would not wish to be remembered by the speakers for his Nobel
Peace Prize, his awards, nor his academic achievements, but
rather for his commitment to social and economic justice for the
oppressed. He said, "Yes, if you want to, say that I was a drum
major. Say that I was a drum major for justice. Say that I was a
drum major for peace. I was a drum major for righteousness."[10]

In contrast and yet in similarity to the preaching of King was
the preaching of the late Reverend Dr. Joseph H. Jackson, who
served as president of the National Baptist Convention, USA for
twenty-nine years.[11] When King flashed upon the scene and was
catapulted into the leadership role of what was to become the
greatest civil rights movement in this nation's history, Jackson
had already made his mark on the national scene as an African
American leader, a preacher, and an excellent orator.

Both King and Jackson were African American Baptist
preachers. Both were great orators. Before 1961 they were members of the same National Baptist Convention. Both King and
Jackson wanted to achieve social justice for African Americans.
King believed that the way to do so was to disrupt the existing
social order through massive nonviolent protests, which would
bring about rapid and radical social change. Jackson believed
that the way to achieve social justice was through cooperation
with the existing social system, which would lead to gradual
liberty and justice for all. This led to conflict between the two
leaders.

It was widely held that the tension between them was height-
ened by the emerging popularity of King as a national and
international leader of the "Negro" community, which de-
tracted from the popularity of Jackson's leadership.

I discuss the practical theology and practical preaching of
these two men because of their leadership, visibility, and massive following during that era. Their beliefs and proclamations
are indelible in the annals of African American history.

From the beginning of the civil rights movement, with the
massive bus boycott in Montgomery, Alabama, and the massive

nonviolent protests that spread like wildfire across the nation, there emerged a contrast in the preaching of King and Jackson.[12] The preaching of both was based on and articulated a practical theology of redemption for the oppressed. The goal was the same—equal rights for the Negroes in America. But, these two men preached diametrically opposed approaches to achieving deliverance for the captives, liberation for the bound, and healing for those who were bruised by the brutality of the oppressors.

In his sermonic annual address of September 1965, Jackson condemned King's method of public, nonviolent, massive protest.[13] He discussed the matter of method:

> We cannot and we must not adopt any methods in our quest for civil rights that may also be used by saboteurs to weaken the nation's life and lower its morale. We must not use those methods that can be employed to carry on un-American activities in the name of freedom or that may be used to overthrow the nation itself or that are in strict violation of the just laws of the land. . . . We must not employ methods that can ruin the lives of those who use them, create more problems than they solve, engender more ill-will than goodwill, and do more to harm our social order than to help it.[14]

(King's detractors had labeled him a Communist or a Communist sympathizer, which was a damaging indictment in those troubled days.)

Throughout his continued career as president of the National Baptist Convention, Jackson maintained that the weapon of nonviolent protest employed by King was not the way to achieve the goal of self-respect and dignity for African Americans. A subsection of his annual address of September 1977 was titled: "From Protest to Production."[15] By then, Jackson had accepted the need as well as the right to protest the evils that would deny any American the "God-given" rights to which all citizens were entitled. But he preached that protest was not enough and he continued his argument that blacks must move from protest to production.

In an earlier sermon, however, we see the same theological background and mandate that we find in King's preaching. Jackson drew inspiration from and made application of the words of Caleb of the Old Testament: "Caleb stilled the people before Moses, and said, Let us go up at once, and possess it; for we are well able to overcome it" (Numbers 13:30, KJV). He edified the audience:

> We *are able* to cope with the moral requirements of freedom as we at the same time struggle to make our nation more just and more free. . . . We *are able* to live while we are dying, to sing while we are suffering, and to trust while we are threatened and tortured by tormentors and by those who would destroy us. We *are able* to break the old chains of servitude, to drop the shackles of superstition, and to free our minds and souls from the dark shadows of oppression and discrimination.[16]

The similarity in the preaching of King and Jackson was a similarity of goal—redemption for the Negroes in America. In 1971 Jackson said: "We must now embrace the fact of our ability and employ it for self-fulfillment, self-growth, and the moral and spiritual redemption of our social order."[17] Both King and Jackson accepted redemption as a divine mandate.

The contrast of the preaching of King and Jackson was a contrast of method to be employed in achieving the desired God-ordained goal. The contrast in views concerning the method to be employed represents the two extreme philosophical poles of the spectrum. All preaching on methods of deliverance of the captives in the African American community has fallen somewhere between these two poles.

There have always been some fundamentalists among the African American pastor-theologians whose preaching focused on personal salvation, spiritualizing, otherworldliness, and noninvolvement in the struggle for human rights in this world. They were so otherworldly focused that they were no thisworldly good. However, this group has always been in the minority, and I have opted to reserve discussion of its theological and preaching tradition for some future time.

Two conclusions are drawn from the King/Jackson theology and preaching. First, freedom from oppression and equal justice for all African Americans as well as for whites are birthrights bestowed by the Creator. When these rights are taken away from one group by another group of individuals who traffic in greed and power, the victims have not only the right but also the responsibility to become involved in activities to rid themselves of the burdens of oppression.

For King, this meant public civil disobedience and nonviolently breaking the unjust laws of segregation supported by city, state, and national legislators, executives, and courts. King's method did prick the nation's conscience, and the walls of physical segregation and separation did come tumbling down.

For Jackson, the way to throw off oppression was to affirm the elusive "American Dream" of achieving civil rights by engaging in economic self-help programs and entrepreneurship, which would evolve into economic parity of blacks with whites. Organizing self-help institutions and engaging in "production" did have some positive results for African Americans after the Civil War and at other periods in African American history. While some African Americans did attempt to achieve redemption by Jackson's method, from the beginning of the civil rights movement clearly the majority of African Americans knew that this approach was inadequate, so they elected to follow the more comprehensive approach preached by King.

Jackson failed to recognize the systemic and structural racism that was inherent in the American economic system, which renders his method ineffective even to this day. A study conducted by the Baltimore Unemployment Council targeted six local banks to determine their compliance with the Community Reinvestment Act. The study confirmed the conclusion reached earlier by the Federal Reserve System that banks in Baltimore rejected black mortgage applicants twice as often as whites.[18] This is just one current example of the inequity that is inherent in the economic system. African Americans have not been able to move ahead meaningfully in the arena of production because of the systematic denial of capital. Preaching must inspire people to become productive, but it must also expose and challenge the unjust system that denies access to the means that make production possible.

A second conclusion to be drawn from the King/Jackson theology and preaching has to do with the methodological approaches followed by the two. The different approaches show that, like other groups in America, African Americans have not been monolithic in their approach to solving the problems of social injustices. But out of the richness of diversity, African

Americans have made steady progress toward the achievement of their divine birthrights in America. There are still setbacks after setbacks, but the tide of divine justice and righteousness still flows in the direction of freedom and justice for all.

While other institutions have come and gone, many of which have served as major catalysts leading the fight for the civil rights of exploited African Americans, the church has been the one institution that has been in the forefront of the movement and must continue to be in the days ahead. The pastor-theologians have been the prime movers in the church and must be the primary drum majors in the future.

It is well known in the African American religious community that a strained relationship existed between King and Jackson. The reasons are many and varied. Both of these men were giants as pastor-theologians. Both achieved national and international attention. In general, King was supported by the white "liberals" while Jackson was supported by the white "conservatives." This had the effect of a "divide and conquer" tactic by those in power. It worked to the degree that some energy was wasted in the attacks and counterattacks by these two factions. This energy could have been used in the redemption movement against the real enemy of social justice.

Two manifestations of the strained relationship of these men were: One, when the Progressive National Baptist Convention was formed in 1961, King, with others, left the National Baptist Convention and became a member of the Progressive Convention. Two, after the assassination of King in April 1968, when the National Baptist Convention met in Atlanta, Georgia, that same year, Jackson did not program a memorial service for King, even though we met in the city of his birth.

In spite of the difference in philosophies of these two men, both espoused a practical theology through their practical preaching. Both used the narrative/storytelling approach in their preaching. This was the approach used by most African American preachers.

Telling the Story

The homileticians have divided sermons into several categories: (1) the textual sermon, in which the text is the theme and the various parts of the text form the main divisions of the sermon; (2) the topical sermon, in which the text suggest the subject and several other texts are used to support the topic; (3) the expository sermon, in which the text is the theme and the whole sermon is an exposition of that theme; and (4) the inferential sermon, in which the theme is inferred in the text but not specifically stated.

James Earl Massey, in his classic book *Designing the Sermon*, advanced three categories of sermon designs: the narrative/story sermon; the textual/expositional sermon; and the doctrinal/topical sermon.[19]

All of these approaches are used in African American preaching, but the narrative/story form has been the one most used in the African American preaching tradition. The question most asked by laypersons when they make inquiries about the ability of a preacher is not whether he or she can explain the propositions implied in the various biblical texts but rather, "Can the preacher tell the story?" That is, can the preacher make plain the truths contained in the text in such a story form that the hearers may be helped, healed, and empowered?

It was this sincere and dramatic way of preaching that led Ray to declare that the black churches were built largely upon preachers who could tell the Bible story. He said in 1970 that some preachers were calling their congregations together for dialogue "because the crowd was falling off" and this was a "method to try to get the crowd out so that the people could participate in the dialogue. But when you tell a story, a true story, there is no dialogue in the story."[20] The characters in the story are involved in dialogue, but the audience does not become engaged in critiquing and evaluating the validity of the story; they are to become involved in the truth of the story.

The African American preaching tradition had its genesis in an oral tradition—preaching from memory and generally without notes. The earliest preachers among African Americans were successors to the griots and storytellers of their African ancestors. For our African ancestors, storytelling was the equivalent of a Western fine art.

In some instances, our society equates illiterature—the absence of the written source—with illiteracy, and illiteracy is equated with inferiority. To the contrary, the ability of the griots, the tribal chiefs, and the storytellers displayed superior intelligence on the part of our ancestors. This cultural survival of the African tradition was manifested in the employment of memorized, metrically composed phrases and stories that recalled their history.[21] The preachers recalled the stories of God's intervention in human history in the Old Testament and related those stories to their own slavery, emancipation, and pilgrimage. In many cases, other lines and phrases that directly addressed certain conditions at hand were spontaneously inserted in the stories. This oral tradition is no indication of mediocrity.

A word of caution to the readers and to the preachers of today: There is no attempt here to elevate oral preaching—preaching without a manuscript—over manuscript preaching, or to elevate manuscript preaching over oral preaching. There is a real danger of a lack of cohesion and comprehensiveness in oral preaching, as is exhibited in too many pulpits Sunday after Sunday in the African American churches today. Thus, the practical theological truths contained in the text are not communicated to the hearts of the hearers. On the other hand, too many manuscripts are just written and read rather than preached and heard. When there is a lack of involvement of the preacher in the story, there is a concomitant lack of involvement of the hearers in the story.

Preaching is serious business, and preachers must intensely, with much prayer, seek to discover their best preaching style and spend the rest of their career developing and embellishing that style. There is no easy way to becoming an oral preacher. There is no easy way to become a manuscript preacher. Many preachers will find themselves combining some oral and some manuscript in their preaching style. Preaching is the vehicle of theology, transporting to the hearts of the hearers transcendent truths in the social context of existence.

In my own preaching, I use an outline so that I can move through the story progressively and yet have the freedom to orally proclaim the story without reading from a prepared script. As I have found a method that works for me, each serious searcher for the method that is appropriate for him or her will find one. (I am still refining my style and practicing.)

Those who will be effective preachers in the African American pulpits in the 1990s and on into the twenty-first century must study the methods of the masters. Success in transmitting theological truths will not be dependent upon whether one is an oral preacher or a manuscript preacher or some combination of both. Success will depend on whether the preacher has internalized the truths of the story. It will depend on whether the story has practical theological significance for the hearers. It will depend on whether the story deals with the eternal truth of the Christian message and with the life situation of a people struggling for survival and searching for meaning in a secularized, urbanized, and ghettoized condition.

The African American communities of the past survived and had meaning because their preachers could tell the Bible story in such a way that lives were transformed and spirits were lifted.

Object and Effect of the Practical

The object of practical theology and practical preaching in the African American churches is to provide the faithful with the strength to endure and to survive. It is to give them the courage to act—to participate in God's plan of redemption from human-caused woes in this world—as well as eternal salvation. Practical theology and practical preaching are technical, theological, and homiletical terms, but they contain measurable objectives in the arena of the faithful. Again, it is through practical preaching that this message of hope and redemption is communicated in the marketplace of existence.

An illustration of practical preaching based on practical theology is that of Sandy Ray. This nation was being blown in every direction from the racial unrest of the 1960s. Ray was preaching to preachers who would return to their pulpits to address matters of life and death with those who were caught in the turbulence of the civil rights struggle and the "Black Power" movement. This sermon, "Spiritual Counsel in Carnal Crises," was the story of the shipwreck Paul experienced as a prisoner on his way to Rome to appeal his case before Caesar (see Appendix).

Paul had advised the shipmasters against traveling; they ignored his advice, launched forth, and found themselves in the midst of a terrible storm. Paul, this preacher-prisoner, now became the "pilot," giving orders that provide salvation for the crew and passengers, as the story was dramatized by this master African American preacher:

> This storm represents the shape of our culture. The masters and pilots have ignored the prophets and left "Fair Havens" at their own risk. They have depended upon their skill, and their science, and their computers, and their technology, and their money, and their armies, and their bombs, and their diplomacy, etc. They are insensitive to "The rumor of angels." The preacher is a star gazer, they say. His message is from another world and has no relevance or word to deal with this storm.[22]

Ray gave counsel then to the preachers:

> Before our culture crashes in this turbulence . . . preachers, you must prepare to become pilots. Because the captains and the pilots and the centurions don't know what to do now. Our ship of state is in serious distress. You may have boarded the ship as a prisoner, but the crisis demands that you move to the helm. . . . You must speak to the panic-stricken masters and hopeless people on this ill-fated ship. You, preachers, must see the glimmers of hope amid the gloom of the crisis. You, preachers, must see this mysterious hand of the Almighty God, guiding gales and stabbing these storms. . . .[23]

The object of this practical sermon that Ray delivered to pastor-theologians who would then duplicate it for their parishioners was to sustain, to encourage, and to motivate them to become active participants in the movement of redemption in their local settings.

Was this practical theology and practical preaching effective? The answer might lie in a series of questions: Have the masses of African Americans survived and maintained their sanity in spite of the cruelty of segregation and dehumanization? Have they maintained and enhanced a sense of pride and dignity? Have they been guided to make right choices among alternatives in life-threatening and life-enhancing situations while their backs were against the wall? Have they been inspired to rise up against every form of oppression that robbed them of their personhood and undermined their human dignity? Are they being continually reconciled to God, to themselves, and to others?

The affirmative answer to these questions would reveal the effectiveness of practical theology and practical preaching in the African American church.

This preaching was not narrow and sectarian; the masses of African American preachers tried to proclaim the whole counsel of God. This is the focus of my discussion in the next two chapters.

Chapter 4

Preaching the Whole Counsel: Plan, Identity, and God

"I did not shrink from declaring to you the whole counsel of God" (Acts 20:27, RSV). "I have not fallen short at all of preaching to you the whole counsel of God" (The Modern English Bible: The New Berkeley Version in Modern English). ". . . the complete counsel of God" (Phillips). ". . . God's whole plan" (Weymouth).

Preaching God's Plan

Preaching the whole counsel of God is an undertaking of which no human being can hope to achieve proficiency, yet it is a divine assignment that no preacher can escape.[1] But to preach the whole counsel, the whole will, the whole plan of God, who is equal to the task? Who is worthy? In an informal discussion with one of my colleagues about theology and the immensity of God, he said: "We are just children in kindergarten with A-B-C blocks trying to spell God. How can we who are born in time, live in time, and die in time explain God who was before time, above time, and beyond time?"[2]

This is a concise confession of our human limitations in matters of theology. In the above passage of Scripture, Paul did not mean that he had succeeded in declaring the whole counsel of God but that he had never ceased in struggling to preach the whole counsel of God. In his letter to the Philippians he acknowledged his limitations:

Brethren, I count not myself to have apprehended: but *this* one thing *I do*, forgetting those things which are behind, and reaching forth unto those things which are before, I press toward the mark for the prize of the high calling of God in Christ Jesus (Philippians 3:13-14, KJV).

Again, Paul wrote to the Colossians:

So, naturally, we proclaim Christ! We warn everyone we meet, and we teach everyone we can, all that we know about him, so that, if possible, we may bring every man up to his full maturity in Christ Jesus. This is what I am working at all the time, with all the strength that God gives me (Colossians 1:28-29, Phillips).

Every preacher must strive toward preaching the whole counsel of God. Any failure in attempting to do so is anathema for one who claims to have been called to the preaching ministry. The attempt to preach the whole counsel of God is very evident in the African American preaching tradition.

The advice of the late John Fitzgerald Kennedy is helpful for those who are challenged to preach the whole counsel of God today. In his inaugural address on January 20, 1961, Kennedy outlined his aspirations and plans for the advancement of our nation. Then he stated, "All this will not be finished in the first one hundred days. Nor will it be finished in the first one thousand days, nor in the life of this administration, nor even perhaps in our lifetime on this planet. But let us begin."[3]

Preaching the whole counsel and plan of God is an evolving and dynamic enterprise that began in antiquity with the patriarchs, continued with the prophets, was practiced in the early Christian church, and has been transmitted from generation to generation over two millennia. We can only expect fulfillment in the *eschatos*—the end of time. But not all preachers of all times attempted to preach the whole counsel of God. In submission to the politics of the imperial and colonial powers, academic theologians and pastor-theologians from generation to generation have often preached certain aspects of the counsel of God while overlooking and sometimes outrightly denying other aspects of the whole plan of God. And this preaching had little concrete meaning for those whose backs were against the wall.

For example, Jürgen Moltmann reflected upon two visions of the period between the French Revolution beginning in 1789 and the beginning of World War I and the Russian Revolution in 1917/1918. The two visions were: (1) the "vision of freedom" and (2) "the authoritarian principle." The vision of freedom and an egalitarian society gave impetus for the French Revolution. The authoritarian principle undergirded the European colonial and imperial expansion all over the globe. This authoritarian principle gave rise to a conservative theology that embraced and elevated "God, king, and fatherland" as the central themes of theology.[4]

The major Christian denominations of the nineteenth century did not preach the whole plan of God, which included individual freedom and an egalitarian society. In fact, the major European churches and theologians—both Catholic and Protestant—presented a selected view of the counsel of God. Moltmann said:

> The Calvinist theologian and Prime Minister of the Netherlands, Abraham Kuyper, commended "reformation against revolution": all revolutions are directed against God. Democracy, the sovereignty of the people, liberalism and secularization are diabolical names for the "beast from the abyss" and signs of the outreach of chaos. Revolution against the ruling powers is rebellion against God . . .[5]

This is, in essence, the foundation and limitation of Euro-American theology and Euro-American preaching. God's plan of freedom, equality (human rights), and brotherhood among all persons was conspicuously missing in the preaching of the counsel of God.

It is true that the founding fathers of this nation developed a theology and a preaching of liberation and freedom from the "crown"—the king of England—but, in every way, they supported, politically and theologically, slavery in America and expansionism, imperialism, slavery, and the economic exploitation of peoples around the world. Thus, preaching in white America tended to avoid or to reject that aspect of the counsel of God that had to do with freedom and justice and redemption for all of humanity.

In 1844 Alexander Glennie, rector of All-Saints Parish in

Waccamaw, South Carolina, published a book of sermons that he regularly preached to the "Coloured portion" of his congregation. He made them available, he said, "in the hope that Catechists and religious Masters may find them of some use."[6] The text of sermon IV was, "With good will doing service, as to the Lord, and not to men" (Ephesians 6:7, KJV). From this text, Glennie preached:

> In this part of the word of God, servants are taught with what mind they ought to do their service. They are told to do what is required of them "with good will:" and to do it, "as to the Lord, and not to men."
>
> What a blessed book the Bible is, my brethren! It speaks comfort to all people in every station of life: it shows how every one must live here, so as to please our heavenly Father. . . . Masters are taught in the Bible, how they must rule their servants, and servants how they must obey their masters. Truly this holy word of God is a blessed gift indeed: and how greatly blessed shall we all be, if we diligently seek the help of the Holy Spirit, that we may be "doers of the word and not hearers only!"[7]

This is an American expression of a European theology that justified imperialism, expansionism, colonialism, and slavery. It is herein refined in American theology and preaching. Theology is always shaped by tradition and the social context of existence. Historical Euro-American theology, in the main, has been a sanctioner and blesser of cultural imperialism. Thus, the preaching—the vehicle of transmitting this theology to the masses—has fallen short of preaching the whole plan of God. This preaching failed to address the "this-worldly" redemption for the servants.

Of course, there have always been white theologians and preachers who have attempted to declare the whole counsel of God, including "this-worldly" redemption for the dispossessed. Some white preacher-theologians have supported the cause of civil rights theologically, politically, economically, socially, and physically. Indeed some have paid the ultimate sacrifice alongside African Americans. But even with massive support, such as that given during the civil rights movement in America, this was the exception rather than the rule. There is still in America today systematic and structural exploitation of the poor by those who traffic in greed and power. Such exploitations give rise to the perpetuation and acceleration of a dependent consumer class. These dependent consumers are trapped in the urbanized and ghettoized sections of our nation. They are crammed in overcrowded schools. They lack adequate housing. Their living conditions in general are less than adequate. Their unemployment rate is generally twice as high as the national average. Their setting is conducive to crime and violence.

African American preaching has given and still gives hope in these seemingly hopeless situations. This practical preaching was the vehicle of their practical theology, which has always striven to incorporate the whole counsel of God, including salvation from sin, but also the hope for freedom, justice, and redemption. Beginning in the "invisible church," when blacks were not permitted to gather for worship or any other assembly without a stated number of "respectable white men" present, blacks held secret meetings and worship services. In these meetings, the preachers attempted to declare the whole counsel of God.

As successor to and transmitter of this tradition, Manuel L. Scott Sr., author of *The Gospel for the Ghetto*, preached a sermon titled "The Inviter," with the text coming from Matthew 11:28, "Come unto me, all *ye* that labor and are heavy laden, and I will give you rest"(KJV). Jesus is the Inviter, but who are the invited? Scott said, "something can be gained . . . by pointing out . . . the audience to whom this invitation was first addressed . . ." And in powerful, poetic language, he preached that this audience was:

parked in poverty pockets and
    gathered in ghettos.
They were Jews, second class citizens
    of the Roman Empire. . . .

They were the culturally deprived and the
    socially disadvantaged.
They were underfed, underhoused, and underclothed.
    They were overworked and underpaid.
These citizens were like cogs in other men's
    machines, compelled to be bearers of
    other men's burdens.

> They were moved about like checkers
>   on a board, according to the whims
>   and wishes of the dominant group. . . .
>
> They were the people against whom the
>   institutions were rigged—the courts,
>   the government, the schools, and even
>   the churches.
>   It was
>   people in such a plight, and
>   listeners with such a lot
>   on whose ears the
>   Great Invitation
>   was the first to fall.[8]

Scott, still in poetic form, raised a question with the great prophets of old—Ezekiel, Daniel, Micah, and others. He raised the question with preachers of the New Testament, including Peter and Paul: "Who is the Inviter?" The response from Daniel, as Scott related it, was "He is 'the stone cut out of the mountain without hands' breaking down idol gods and vanishing immoral kingdoms."[9]

In this preaching of the plan of God, first, the listeners could readily identify with those who were invited in the biblical story. Second, they were promised through the prophecy of Daniel that Jesus was the one who would redeem them, not only by atoning for sin, but also by breaking down the kingdoms of the earthly gods and vindicating the hopes of the oppressed.

This was practical preaching based on practical theology addressing the life situation as well as the eternal aspiration of the people. Such a preaching tradition continues to this day. African American preachers have attempted to preach the whole counsel, realizing that its fulfillment is an eschatological notion. Preachers must preach as if this is the end. This preaching tradition unveiled for African Americans a portion of God's plan that had not heretofore been proclaimed among them by their captors. Through the preaching, the people discovered that God was in the struggle with them for redemption—this-worldly as well as otherworldly redemption—liberation from human bondage and the formation of a confederation of the people of God. This confederation meant a people living in a covenant relationship with each other and with God.

Preaching the whole counsel included the telling and retelling of the biblical incidents of God's self-revelation in human history and God's promise and plan for continued involvement in the redemption of his people. Benjamin Brawley put in poetic lines an affirmation of God's redemptive plan:

There Is a Plan
Far above the strife and striving,
And the hate of man for man,
I can see the great contriving
Of a more than human plan.

And day by day more clearly
Do we see the great design,
And day by day more nearly
Do our footsteps fall in line.

For in spite of the winds repeating
The rule of the lash and rod,
The heart of the world is beating
With the love that was born of God.[10]

African American preaching always affirmed a divine plan for human redemption. Who, then, is this character who dares to attempt the preaching of the whole counsel of God?

The Preacher's Identity

"In those days came John the Baptist, preaching . . ." (Matthew 3:1, KJV). John the Baptist was certain of his identity, certain of his call, and certain of his mission. He is a prototype for the African American preacher-preaching tradition.

In an oral insertion in his sermon "The Preacher in the Pastor," Dr. Caesar Clark said that John the Baptist identified himself as just a voice. "John the Baptist was born too late for the prophets and too early for the apostles so he identified himself as just a voice."[11] Like John the Baptist, African American preachers know that they are just town heralds bringing the news from another source. They do not make the news but are the news reporters. They are not editors deleting and adding that which mixes facts with opinions. They are bearers of an eternal message but not the authors of the message that is delivered.

The voice of the preacher becomes the voice of the Eternal. The audacious assignment is to speak for God and about God to the people of God of whom the preacher is just one called out as proclaimer. The preacher is like student to teacher, Clark noted. The teacher instructs the student to "stand up and repeat after me." When the preacher gets up to preach, Jesus says, "repeat after me."[12]

Personal significance of the African American preachers fades into the background of the shadow of the divine message at preaching time. Preachers assure others of their destiny but are not masters of their own destiny. They preach with authority but are under orders from another Authority. They give the Word but are just the servants of that Word. Their title of honor is often reversed with ridicule by some of the hearers as well as outside detractors. But the whole counsel of God, revealed in the proclamation, gives the masses the strength to endure, the courage to struggle against dehumanizing forces, and the power to transcend the human-caused trials and tribulations in countless otherwise hopeless situations.

African American preachers came not only in the tradition of John the Baptist, but also in that of the Old Testament prophets. What Peter T. Forsyth said of the Christian preacher is particularly true of African American preachers: "The Christian preacher is not the successor of the Greek orator, but of the Hebrew prophet. The orator comes with an inspiration; the prophet comes with a revelation."[13]

Certainly, in the African American mass churches—those attended by the masses of common folk—there has been a lot of inspiration. The preaching has been oratorical and replete with artistic beauty. But the intrinsic efficacy in African American preaching of the whole counsel of God has been the revelation often coming in on the wings of the inspiration and celebration. The calling is to reveal God's plan of redemption.

The idea of "call" has always had great theological significance for African American preachers and the elders of the church. Every preacher in the mass African American church was required to ascertain his or her call before the elders of the church. With Paul, they believed that people will not call upon him whom they have not believed, and people can't believe upon him whom they have not heard, and they cannot hear without a preacher, and the preacher can't preach unless the preacher has had a divine call (see Romans 10:13-15, KJV).

The relevance of divine call has been resonant in the African American theology of preaching. And that theology of preaching is the acknowledgment and affirmation that preaching is the divine mandate and medium for communicating, elucidating, and illuminating God's revelation for the people.

The mission of the preacher is to be the bearer of the gospel—the Good News of redemption. In the African American theological preaching tradition, there was always the message of reproach (chastisement for wrongdoing) and threat (the pronouncement of judgment). But the preaching always included a message of exhortation and promise— guidance and hope. So the idea of "How beautiful are the feet of them that preach the gospel of peace, and bring glad tidings of good things" (Romans 10:15, KJV) is of utmost importance. The beauty here, as understood by both African American preachers and people, had nothing to do with the physical feet of the messenger, but rather "How welcome is the coming of those who bring good news" (Goodspeed). The bearer of the whole counsel was on a mission for the Creator to the creatures. And in anticipation of the Good News of the bearer of the message, like the ancient Israelites, African Americans rejoiced at the appearance of the messenger.

Caesar Clark gave a good summary of the identity of the African American preacher when he declared, "We are not to preach ourselves! We are not 'stars.' Preparation precedes preaching! There is a pastor in the preacher and there is a preacher in the pastor! The preacher preaches as an accredited herald of God and as a true shepherd of souls!"[14]

African American preachers, with the aid of the Holy Spirit, knowing their identity as heralds of God and shepherds of the soul, developed the art of trying to preach the whole counsel. By study, observation, and involvement, they developed the tremendous skill of performing the preaching ministry. They developed creativity in the adaptation and application of the message to address the social circumstances of the hearers with eternal interpretations and declarations.

African American preachers are not just ambassadors for God

on a general mission in the world. They are indeed ambassadors to the world in general; but, more particularly, African American preachers preach to a particular people with a particular message of redemption that transcends the meaning of redemption in the larger Christian community. When the feet of the African American preacher ascend to the pulpit on Sunday morning, the message has a theological foundation not based on theory about the counsel of God. The message is anchored in practical theology. The message is a reflection upon the gospel in the light of faith becoming action in the cause of social justice. The preacher is a special person with a special calling, with a special message of hope to a special people from the underside of life in America.

Preaching the Counsel of God

God of Creation

Use of the Bible was central in historical African American preaching. The stories of the God of the Old Testament were told and retold in such a way that the hearers identified themselves with God's people of the Old Testament, and those ancient stories became their stories; the God of the Israelites became their God and their Redeemer.

Preaching became the vehicle of theology, asserting the redemptive events of biblical history. They could never express the full meaning of God, but they expressed many of the attributes of God. These attributes were not taken basically from the theological books; they came down through the oral preaching tradition. They were articulated in sermons Sunday after Sunday. The preachers preached about their God, who was active in the practical life struggles of the people.

The black view of God as Creator was summed up in a poetic sermon by James Weldon Johnson titled "The Creation." In all of African American preaching, this is the best summation of God as Creator. It is a good summary of the understanding of God as Creator prior to its composition, and all succeeding African American preaching about creation and God as Creator is just an extension of this early theological proclamation.[15]

The God Who Takes Off Chariot Wheels

In African American preaching, God is also the Divine Being who intervenes in human history on the side of those in need of redemption from human-caused oppression. Every African American parishioner has heard some form of the oral sermon titled or implied "The God Who Takes Off Chariot Wheels." God is not only Creator, but, after creation, is active in the affairs of human events. God acted on behalf of his people, the Israelites, as they were being pursued by the Egyptians, who had held them in bondage for 430 years. In the midst of the Red Sea, God took off the wheels of the chariots of the oppressors and the Israelites were able to escape.

The story of the "God Who Takes Off Chariots Wheels" provided, and yet provides, great inspiration for a people who were and are the object of exploitation and dehumanization, then on the plantations and now in the ghettos. Preaching about a mighty God who takes off chariots wheels dramatized the all-powerfulness of God in a way that was readily comprehended by the hearers. The creativity in this dramatic preaching was the taking of the incomprehensible and making it plain for the uncomprehending. The power of God is not theory. The power of God is action.

The story of the Israelites' escape from the pursuing army of Pharaoh showed how God divinely intervened on the side of the escaping slaves and how God personally rendered the Egyptian army incapable of further pursuit. Then the almighty God who had opened the Red Sea for the children of Israel acted again through divine power and closed up the sea, drowning Pharaoh's army who had been trapped there by the loss of their chariot wheels.

This was a pictorial, practical theological assertion about the power and omnipotence of the God of the Old Testament, and the hearers were always assured that this God was also their God. The story spoke with great force to the life-threatening situation of the oppressed, giving them hope of survival and overcoming because the same all-powerful, all-caring, and all-acting God would, in time, take off the chariot wheels of their oppressors, rendering them incapable of continual exploitation and oppression.

Other biblical stories that were regularly preached showing

the power of God in rescuing people would include that of the deliverance of Daniel from the lions' den, the deliverance of the Hebrew children from the fiery furnace, and the deliverance of Paul and Silas from imprisonment in the jail in Philippi. The extent of the telling and the dramatization of these and similar stories are too well known in the African American religious community to warrant further documentation at this point.

So this preaching about the power—the omnipotence—of God was not abstract and esoterical. It was not a theoretical and obscure notion. The idea of the power of the almighty God was demonstrated through the stories of God's concern for people and intervention in human history as Redeemer of the oppressed. It was directly applicable to the African American life situation. This was a practical theology. "The Moses story"—his call, the Exodus, the wilderness, and the Canaan experience—was and is a major theological theme in African American preaching.

The God of the Bible and thus the God of African Americans is Creator, is all-powerful, acts on the side of the downtrodden, and is ever present in the midst of the people.

The God of Presence

The late Reverend Dr. William R. Haney titled one of his sermons "Communicating Experience with God." His biblical text was, "Come *and* hear, all ye that fear God, and I will declare what he hath done for my soul" (Psalm 66:16, KJV).[16]

Throughout this sermon, Haney inspired the listeners with the fact that God has always been present with his people. This was not one of the attributes of God to be cognized by the listeners; he simply showed how this theological truth was manifested in the experience of the Israelites' sojourn.

Of verses 5-7 of Psalm 66 he said: ". . . The nations are invited to take cognizance of the mighty acts of God in the history of the Chosen People." The two acts to which he called attention were the crossing of the Red Sea—the Exodus—and the crossing of the Jordan (Joshua 3). These and subsequent events, he said, show how God keeps watch over the nation. The point here is that the God who is Creator is the God who keeps constant watch over the people.

The idea that God is ever watching over the people is far more profound for the laity than to say that God is omnipresent. In fact, Haney dramatized how the psalmist said in verse 5, "Come and see the works of God . . .": "He calls all . . . who fear God" to come and hear the testimonies of the witnesses to God's goodness.

"Facts are facts," Haney declared. "The world can understand a fact far better than a theory."[17] In this worship setting, Haney called for a practical rather than a theoretical understanding of the meaning of the presence of God in the life experience of the Israelites. This was practical theology and practical preaching.

Of the psalmist, he declared, "Here is a man who has a story to tell that simply will not keep."[18] He amplified this idea from the New Testament by pointing out that as soon as Andrew and Philip found the Messiah, they brought the news to Peter and Nathaniel, and how when the Samaritan woman was convinced that Jesus was the Messiah, she invited the whole city to come and see the Person whom she believed to be the Christ.

"These are facts," declared the preacher. They are stories of the appearances and presence of the divine in human history that "simply would not keep."

In the first of the three divisions of this sermon, Haney discussed the theme of the psalmist. The psalmist, he said, was not attracting attention to get a forum to discuss the matter in the marketplace. He was not calling the people together to discuss ancient or modern literature, nor to discuss the latest scientific discoveries. All of these are important in some setting but not in this preaching context. Haney declared that the psalmist ". . . is not telling his theories or his hope. He is not engaging in a theological discussion." The psalmist was rather bringing a sure word from God. It was a sure word of a personal relationship with God.[19] It was a true story to be shared, not a theory to be discussed or debated. Of course, the listeners could readily internalize the psalmist's story and make it their own.

In the second division of the sermon, Haney raised a question, "What is the story?" What has God done for the psalmist and/or his people? The answers: First, God answers prayer in human situations. Second, the psalmist had learned the approach to God. "This psalmist," Haney said, "has not succeeded in opening the door to that audience chamber where the soul and God stand face-to-face only to forget the combination, and never be able to return again."[20] The point was that God is always present, and again and again the soul can come face-to-face with God through prayer. Third, it is always a thrilling experience to get an answer to prayer. This is the new sense of God that comes to those who pray effectively. In summary, the story was a theological one; it was a story of another dimension of the counsel of God; it was a story of the presence of the Divine and of successive encounters with the eternal God.

The third division of the sermon raised two questions: "Why does the psalmist tell his story?" and "Why do we tell our story?" First, Haney suggested, the story was told from necessity. "Why is a rose red?" he asked. "Not because it wants to blush for pleasure, but because it is the nature of the rose to be red. Why does Niagara Falls thunder?" It is not to put on a show to amuse the tourists. "It cannot help thundering."[21] It is the nature of the waterfall to thunder. Likewise for the psalmist and for those of us who have encountered God in the soul and in history, it is our nature to tell the story from necessity. We tell the story as an expression of our inherent nature.

Second, we tell the story, he said, because we are commanded to do so. And third, we tell the story from the inner urge that is characteristic of all who "have come into possession of vital knowledge of God."[22]

Three years earlier, preaching before the same group, Haney used the text, "He said, 'My presence will go with you, and I will give you rest'" (Exodus 33:14, RSV). Here God's word of assurance was a response to the anticipated concern of Moses: "... If thy presence will not go with me, do not carry us up from here" (verse 15). The topic of this sermon was "The Promise of God's Presence."[23] God's presence was significant for Moses in his continued leadership of God's people through the wilderness. In fact, Moses' statement reflected that he would rather continue wandering in the wilderness with God than to move on without God's presence. It is better to be where one is with God than to go where one is without God. Haney addressed three major points in this sermon: One, the presence of God on an unfamiliar road is better than advance knowledge of the way ahead—"Show me the way." Two, divine presence means divine companionship and the experience of God's friendship—"Show me thy glory." Three, God's presence is more than an "afterglow of transcendent glory"—"I will give you rest." This is rest in the midst of toil.[24] This is not just glory; it is tranquility in the midst of adversity.

These two sermons had much in common; they reflected the redemptive journey of the Israelites; the presence of God with them, and their success under the mighty hand of God. Haney had gathered up the biblical stories as preached in the bush arbors, the wooden churches of the South, and the storefronts and sanctuaries of the urban ghettos. He refined those stories and preached them anew to preachers who would return to the rurals of the South and the ghettos of the North to preach them to their parishioners anew. The theological truths revealed what God has done in the past, is doing in the present, and will do in the future for his people. This was not theory; this was preaching based on practical theology. This was preaching God's presence.

The God of Justice

The story of the call and message of the prophet Amos has been heard in one form or another again and again in black churches around the nation. The reason is that the theme of justice for the poor permeates the prophecy of Amos and has been at the center of African American preaching.

When African American preacher-theologians preached the Amos story, the listeners identified the preacher with Amos and themselves with the suffering poor of that day. Amos's God became their God, the God who calls the prophet to demand justice for the poor.

Those who trafficked in greed and power in Amos's day were keeping so-called religious feasts and solemn assemblies, but these were rejected by God. African Americans, hearing the preaching of the Amos story, identified the oppressors of that day with the oppressors of their day. They were religious in rituals but void in righteousness. In their overt clamor for material wealth, ". . . they sold the righteous for silver, and the poor for a pair of shoes" (Amos 2:6, KJV).

Amos was a peasant of Tekoa. He was a shepherd/herdsman. He was a dresser of sycamore trees. Amos was called to be God's spokesman on behalf of the poor in a time of material prosperity of the oppressors in the midst of graft and greed, crime and corruption, and religious formalities. In this context of suffering, Amos was preacher-theologian. To the exploiters, he pronounced God's judgment for their transgressions. To the poor, he preached "The Day of the Lord." The Day of the Lord was to be a day of judgment for the oppressors, but it would be a day of redemption for the oppressed.

It is little wonder that African Americans have followed and rallied around their various religious leaders as they have emerged on the American scene. Such leaders included Denmark Vesey, Booker T. Washington, Mary McLeod Bethune, Harriett Tubman, Sojourner Truth, Marcus Garvey, Malcolm X, Martin Luther King Jr., and others. These were the successors to Amos of the Old Testament.

It was no coincidence that in his "I Have a Dream" speech before two hundred thousand at the Lincoln Memorial in Washington, D.C., on August 28, 1963, King said:

> There are those who ask the devotees of civil rights, "When will you be satisfied?" We can never be satisfied as long as the Negro is the victim of the unspeakable horrors of police brutality. . . . We can never be satisfied as long as our children are stripped of their selfhood and robbed of their dignity by signs stating "For Whites Only." . . . No, no, we are not satisfied, and we will not be satisfied until justice rolls down like waters and righteousness like a mighty stream.[25]

The last sentence of this statement came from Amos 5:24, but this is a familiar theme preached regularly in African American pulpits around the nation. King was preaching directly from the African American tradition. And African Americans of this religious tradition could readily identify with the theological implication in the preaching: social justice is a divine mandate and the approaching "Day of the Lord" would be a day of judgment for the oppressors and a day of redemption for the oppressed. The Day of the Lord did come in one sense. The walls of social segregation did crumble. But the problem of economic deprivation still persists.

The Amos story is still a very popular theme in African American churches today, particularly since African Americans are becoming more urbanized and more ghettoized, with fewer and fewer economic resources. America still has a way to go in eradicating the structural and systemic oppression that makes social justice an illusion for African Americans.

Preachers of the whole counsel of God do not stand in their own authority, but they, like children before their teacher, follow Jesus' instruction when he says, "Stand up and repeat after me." These preachers realize that God defies definition, but, like children with A-B-C blocks, they attempt to spell God with each sermon, knowing that the whole counsel of God can only be fully disclosed in the *eschatos*.

In this chapter, we have discussed preaching God's plan, the preacher's identity, and the counsel of God. However, preaching the whole counsel of God also means preaching Jesus—God the Son—and preaching God the Holy Ghost—"The Fire Next Time." This is the focus of the following chapter.

Chapter 5

Preaching the Whole Counsel: Jesus and the Fire Next Time

I indeed baptize you with water unto repentance: but he that cometh after me is mightier than I, whose shoes I am not worthy to bear: he shall baptize you with the Holy Ghost, and *with* fire: (Matthew 3:11, KJV).

Preaching Jesus

John the Baptist came baptizing with water, but he declared that when Jesus came, he would be baptizing with the Holy Ghost and with fire. Jesus in African American preaching is Christ—the promised Messiah. However, the faithful have come to know that he is who he is because he did what he did. In the Old Testament, God is the Great "I AM." When Moses asked, ". . . When I come unto the children of Israel . . . and they . . . say to me, What *is* his name? what shall I say unto them?" God responded, "I AM THAT I AM . . . Thus shalt thou say unto the children of Israel, I AM hath sent me unto you" (Exodus 3:13-14, KJV).

Jesus is the "I AM." Gardner C. Taylor, a dean of preachers, titled one of his sermons "A Great New Testament 'I Am.'"[1] His text was: "I am the door: by me if any man enter in, he shall be saved, and shall go in and out, and find pasture" (John 10:9, KJV). In this sermon, Taylor preached Jesus as the "I AM." While God the Father is still central in theology and preaching in the African American churches, Jesus becomes the fulfillment of the "I AM" of the Old Testament in a very concrete way in the lives of the people. African American congregants hear and identify with many sermons revealing Jesus as the "I AM": "I am the bread of life"; "I am the light of the world"; "I am the good shepherd"; "I am the resurrection and the life"; "I am the way, the truth, and the life"; "I am meek and lowly in heart"; "I am the Alpha and the Omega."

Taylor was right; Jesus is the great New Testament "I AM," particularly for African Americans. Taylor rightfully preached that Jesus is the door, the opening, the passageway, and the grand entrance into life itself. Jesus is the way to God. Through him we have access to the Father. He is the new and living Way. But Taylor also depicted Jesus as the door through which African Americans pass in order to reach earthly objectives:

> How many of us have had to stand looking at doors beyond which were the things we needed, yet we were denied the right to go through the door? Some may not go through the door of registering and voting, but I could tell you of fearful and dangerous times when people risked their lives to try to get that door opened for black people. Some I knew died in the effort.[2]

The first theological implication in the text and in the sermon was that, by divine plan, everyone has the privilege to enter the door to salvation, here and hereafter, which is Jesus Christ. Second, those who do enter shall be saved. For African Americans, *saved* has the extended meaning of freedom in this world as well as a haven in the world to come.

Save has a soteriological, or salvation, meaning here that includes redemption from the Fall in Eden and the consequential sin of all humanity. But Taylor pointed the listeners to the Phillips translation of that verse, which tends to back the theology of this statement out of the future and into the present. This was comforting for the listeners. It reads "I am the door. If a man goes in through me, he will be safe and sound; he can come in and out and find his food." For African Americans, this translation, although not changing the soteriological meaning of being *saved* from "the Fall, sin, and eternal ruin," extends the meaning. It moves the meaning of salvation from the otherworldly and backs it into this world. It moves the story out of the *eschatos*—the end time—into the existential—the now. It is this dimension of soteriology—salvation in Jesus

Christ—that sets African American soteriology apart from white soteriology.

Jesus addresses the real-life situation of the hearers. "If a man goes in through me, he will be safe and sound" is good news now for those who stand at a time in history with their backs against the walls of segregation, starvation, exploitation, and dehumanization. Jesus is the "I AM" of the Old Testament whose presence is always with his people.

Safety in Jesus, however, does not exempt Christians from the burdens of difficult experiences in life. "It means rather 'a safe in,' not a 'safe from,' whatever may happen."[3] This theology and preaching has been the mainstay of African Americans. It is this theological truth—"safe in the arms of Jesus"—that has kept African Americans from going mad in their struggle for freedom in America.

Further, to "find food" has been interpreted to mean the finding of spiritual food, but, for the African American pastor-theologian, this text also has a practical application, and that practical application would be declared in the sermon and internalized by the listeners. It means that through Jesus one's earthly needs will be supplied.

Jesus is "I Am," which means for African Americans that he is also Father. In the mainline African American church, there has never been any major debate about Jesus' identity with God. Jesus is God and God is Jesus. This theological truth has been preached in the churches down through the years. A primary text on this important subject is:

> Philip said to him, "Lord, show us the Father, and we will be satisfied." Jesus said to him, "Have I been with you all this time, Philip, and you still do not know me? Whoever has seen me has seen the Father. How can you say, 'Show us the Father'?" (John 14:8-9, NRSV).

"A Human Request and a Divine Reply" is the title of another sermon by Taylor to address this matter. It is typical of preaching Jesus as Father.[4] The preacher moved through the discussion that Jesus had with his disciples:

> Do not let your hearts be troubled. Believe in God, believe also in me. . . . I go and prepare a place for you. . . I will come

again. . . . No one comes to the Father except through me. If you know me, you will know my Father also. From now on you do know him and have seen him (John 14:1-7, NRSV).

In this powerful, interpretative, and declarative sermon, Taylor put it this way:

So! When Jesus said that people knowing Him should know the Father, also, Philip thought the time had come to straighten out a matter which had bothered him for a long time. Was Jesus saying that He pointed to God in His teachings? Was He saying that He, Jesus, somehow symbolized God? To Philip it was all too important a matter to be left in limbo, vague, murky, not clear. So Philip cried out, blurted forth, put to Jesus as natural a human request as human lips can ever utter, "Lord, show us the Father, and we will be satisfied" (John 14:8, RSV).[5]

With this, Taylor said that we must admit that Philip's request is the desire of our hearts. Then he added, "I join my heart and voice to Philip's—'Lord, shew us the Father.'"[6]

To Philip's human request, Jesus gave a divine reply: "He that hath seen me hath seen the Father." The preacher declared to his audience that:

This is the bedrock of the faith of Christian believers. We have seen God in the face of Jesus Christ. He is all the God we need. In Christ, Father God is come down out of the clouds and tabernacles *to where you and I live* (emphasis added). In Jesus, Father God has made Himself forever visible. In Jesus Christ, Father God has visited His lost and wandering children in a far country. . . . Christ tells us and shows us that God goes "about doing good." God in Christ heals the sick and raises the dead, gives an extra vision to the sightless, and lets deaf people hear the music of the spheres. God in Christ visits families that are mourning and sits down at feasts with those who rejoice.[7]

This was preaching and practical theology at its best. It was a clear interpretation of who Jesus is. Jesus is God. This is the foundation of the Christian faith. But he is not God residing in the distant clouds and tabernacles somewhere in the sky. He is God the Father who comes down to "where you and I live." It has always been important for African American Christians to be reassured that Jesus lives where they live, amid all of the contradictions and consternations of life. Taylor, being a master pastor-theologian, gave a model sermon of our God who is so vast that he defies definition. With our A-B-C blocks, however, we can spell Jesus, and he is God with us in our daily struggles.

In this sermon, Taylor brought God through Jesus Christ into the far country of his wandering children. He brought God into the rooms of those who were sick, into the doctor's office of those with visual or hearing impairments. He brought God into the halls of those families who were mourning and into the churches where others were at worship and celebration. The listeners knew, too, that God in Jesus Christ came to make provisions for the poor. This is an important theological concept for African Americans. ". . . God was in Christ, reconciling the world unto himself" (2 Corinthians 5:19, KJV). And he is also God the active Redeemer in human history. This may be an extension of the whole counsel of God in Jesus Christ not readily preached in the majority culture.

"Shall We Look for Another," is the title of a sermon preached by the late S. Leon Whitney. The well-known text was:

> Now when John had heard in the prison the works of Christ, he sent two of his disciples, And said unto him, Art thou he that should come, or do we look for another? (Matthew 11:2-3, KJV)[8]

In this sermon, Whitney pointed out that John had carried out his assignment. John had been the voice of hope in the dark and bleak world of his day. John was imprisoned for his moral standard of preaching, which flew in the face of the rulers of his day. Shut away in jail, John was puzzled, troubled, and alone. So he began to wonder about the Messiah. "Did I make a mistake? Why am I in jail?"[9]

At this point, Whitney began to apply the lesson to the life situation of the hearers. "Many people are asking this question ['Should we look for another?'], though they ask it not verbally. This question is being asked in our social affairs." Then he asserted, "There is nothing wrong with America that Christ cannot straighten out."[10] The preaching then took the story out of antiquity and applied it in a practical way to the life situation of the audience.

God may not always bring us out of the jails we find ourselves in for carrying out the work that he has assigned to us, Whitney noted. "But one thing that all of us know, God is able to make us safe from the ills of life. . . . The God who holds this world in His hands is able to deliver those whom He chooses to deliver."[11]

At the end of the sermon, this African American settled the theological questions in the pulpit that some have not been able to settle in the seminaries: "By what means do you get to know who Jesus was?" "Did he do what he did because he was who he was, or do we know that he was who he was because he did what he did?" Whitney pointed to Jesus' response to the question of John's disciples, "Art thou the Christ, or do we look for another?":

> Jesus told the disciples to tell John the dead is raised, the blind can now see, the deaf can now hear, the captives are at liberty. Tell John that things are not the way they used to be. Tell John that Adam is no longer lost, that the link between earth and heaven is now reconnected.[12]

Here the preacher made two cogent points: First, John would recognize that Jesus was who he was because he did what he did, and the people of the church would now know, too. Jesus did not answer, "Yes, I am the Messiah"; he just pointed to what he did.

Second, the preacher affirmed that Jesus not only set the captives free and gave sight to the blind and hearing to the deaf. Jesus also broke the yoke of sin caused by Adam and made the reconnection between the Creator in heaven and the human creatures on earth. This was powerful practical theology. Here the ministry of Jesus was not abstract and esoterical; it was the practical interpretation of what God has done through Jesus Christ.

Who is Jesus Christ? He is God. How do the masses learn that Jesus is God? They learn this from the preaching of the pastor-theologian. He is not a God out yonder. He is God in our midst. The universal becomes localized in Jesus and resides in the local community. All of the presence and promise of the God of the Old Testament were fulfilled in Jesus of Nazareth.

Jesus is "I AM." Jesus is the door. And Jesus is God. These are just glimpses of Jesus in the counsel of God as preached in the African American churches. When his personal departure was imminent, he promised that his Father would send another Comforter who would abide with humankind forever. Preaching the whole counsel of Jesus Christ leads naturally to the preaching of the whole counsel of the Holy Ghost.

Preaching the Fire Next Time: The Holy Ghost

It is ingenious how the African American fathers and mothers in the preaching ministry could pull together the biblical stories, combine them, and formulate theological truths that were first proclaimed from the pulpits and then transformed into songs by the congregations. One such theological statement and song is "The Fire Next Time." The preachers combined the story of Noah in Genesis 6-9, which concluded with God making a covenant promising that he would not destroy the world by water/flood anymore, with other biblical stories of fire and brimstone, such as found in Luke 17:29: "The same day that Lot went out of Sodom it rained fire and brimstone from heaven, and destroyed *them* all" (KJV). The African American preachers proclaimed "The Fire Next Time," and they created a song in poetic lines:

> And God showed Noah
> the rainbow sign.
> It won't be water,
> but fire next time. [13]

It is from this song, I believe, that James Baldwin borrowed the title for his book *The Fire Next Time*. It was first published in 1964 and was in its ninth printing by 1969. In it, Baldwin discussed the gruesome details of brutality, exploitation, and oppression of the "Negroes" in Harlem, New York, and in the "cities of destruction" around the nation.[14] His conclusion was:

> If . . . the relatively conscious whites and the relatively conscious blacks . . . do not falter in our duty now, we may be able, handful that we are, to end the racial nightmare, and achieve our country, and change the history of the world. If we do not now dare everything, the fulfillment of that prophecy, recreated from the Bible in song by a slave, is upon us: God gave Noah the rainbow sign, No more water, the fire next time![15]

Baldwin was talking about the eruptions of civil unrest and civil disobedience that did take place in America and still take place today in the "cities of destruction." Structural and systemic exploitation arising out of racism, greed, and the clamor for power makes the prediction of "fire next time" future as well as past and present.

African American preaching in the present and future, as in the past, has the awesome task of speaking comfort and hope to the exploited while at the same time demanding relief and justice from the exploiters as a divine mandate.

Not water, but fire next time, as understood in the African American religious community, also has another meaning. Fire can be destructive and devastating, but it can also be comforting and healing, as in the case of the baptism with fire of which John the Baptist spoke in Matthew 3:11.

Again, the African American preacher-theologians had a special God-given ability to take the words once spoken, as recorded in Holy Scripture, making new theological formations and making them speak fresh again in the ears of a distraught people who had not attained social justices. Baptism of the Holy Spirit is another comforting manifestation of God with God's people.

However, the mainline African American denominations—those emerging out of or breaking away from the mainline Protestant denominations, particularly the Baptists and the variety of Methodist groups—did not develop a clear doctrine of the Holy Spirit that was communicated to the practitioners through practical preaching. They did develop the doctrine of God the Father and God the Son. One reason for the absence of the preaching on the Holy Spirit is that these African American denominations had their roots in the doctrines already developed by their predecessor denominations. These doctrines were reinterpreted by the African Americans in their emerging churches prior to and for the next several decades after the Civil War, but they, like their predecessors, did not give much attention to the doctrine of the Holy Spirit. Thus, the Holy Spirit was not prevalent in the preaching.

Some segments of the mainline Protestant denominations held that the reality of the Holy Spirit being manifest in signs and wonders, physical healing, prophecy, and tongues was limited to the age of the apostles and the early Christian church. They held that such manifestations were evident in the early church to authenticate the apostles but that the age of signs and wonders and prophecy passed with the passing of those individuals. The mainline African American churches followed the mainline white Protestant churches on this doctrine and thus there was a void in preaching the whole counsel of God as it related to the Holy Spirit. This is what the preaching was in general, but there were always some exceptions.

In his post-Resurrection and pre-Ascension statement, Jesus instructed his disciples "not to leave Jerusalem, but to wait there for the promise of the Father. . . . 'for John baptized with water, but you will be baptized with the Holy Spirit. . . . You will receive power when the Holy Spirit has come upon you; and you will be my witnesses . . .'" (Acts 1:4-8, NRSV).

The early disciples did have power, and they did witness in at least three ways: First, they witnessed through their testimonies. Second, they witnessed through their sincere caring for the well-being of one another and for others. Third, they witnessed by the liberal sharing of their resources.

While there has been little attention given to this doctrine of the Holy Spirit in liberation theology, there is no lack of the presence of the Holy Spirit in the black church tradition. And this is why the African American theologians must discuss the Holy Spirit, noted J. Deotis Roberts.[16]

James Forbes, writing from a new Pentecostal perspective said, "I came to characterize our style of ministry as 'progressive pentecostalism'—a strong emphasis on spirit, but a deep commitment to transformative social action."[17] African American theologians and preachers must discuss the Holy Spirit, and we must incorporate the "progressive pentecostalism" idea advanced by Forbes with emphasis on the Spirit and a commitment to a transformed social action. We must be committed to preaching the whole counsel.

I offer three reasons for preaching the whole counsel of the Holy Spirit—God's whole plan for the operation of the Holy Spirit in the lives of individuals, in the corporate body of believers, and in the world.

First, the Holy Spirit is promised in the Old Testament. The way to begin to understand the biblical meaning of the Holy

Spirit is not to start with the book of Acts, chapter 2. When we are building a Christology, we begin in the Old Testament. Among other passages, we always refer to Isaiah's pronouncements:

> Unto us a child is born, unto us a son is given: and the government shall be upon his shoulder: and his name shall be called Wonderful, Counsellor, The mighty God, The everlasting Father, The Prince of Peace (Isaiah 9:6, KJV).

We also turn to Isaiah 53:1-5: "Who hath believed our report? . . . For he shall grow up before him as a tender plant. . . . He was despised and rejected. . . . Surely he hath born our griefs. . . . But he was wounded for our transgressions . . ." As we turn to the Old Testament for the grounding of Christology, we must turn there for the grounding of pneumatology, or the beginning of the counsel of the Holy Spirit.

In Numbers 11:16-30, God instructed Moses to call together the seventy elders upon whom he would put some of the spirit that he had already put upon Moses. This was to equip the elders to assist Moses in the ministry of leadership. After they had carried out the commandment and the spirit had been put upon the elders, they began to prophesy. Two of the elders prophesied in the camp rather than in the tent. A complaint came to Moses, who said to leave them alone, but then Moses made a special prayer: "Would that all the LORD's people were prophets, and that the LORD would put his spirit on them" (Numbers 11:29, NRSV). Note well that spirit is always put upon, poured out, or poured into people to impel them to do something. It is never *just* to make them ecstatic. It is not *just* to make them "happy." It is not *just* to make them speak in tongues.

Then we turn to the prophecy of Joel, through whom God spoke:

> Then afterward I will pour out my spirit on all flesh; your sons and your daughters shall prophesy, your old men shall dream dreams, and your young men shall see visions. Even on the male and female slaves in those days will I pour out my spirit (Joel 2:28-29, NRSV).

Peter declared that this prophecy was being fulfilled in the experience on the day of Pentecost (Acts 2:14-21).

The Old Testament contains many references to the pouring out or the sending of the Holy Spirit, including Isaiah 32:15: "until a spirit from on high is poured out on us . . ." and Isaiah 44:3: ". . . I will pour my spirit upon your descendants, and my blessing on your offspring" (NRSV). So to begin to understand the Holy Spirit, we would start in the same place that we started in our attempt to understand Jesus Christ, that is, in the Old Testament. We should preach the whole counsel of the Holy Spirit because he is promised in the Old Testament.

Second, we must realize, then, that the Holy Spirit is promised in the Old Testament as a third manifestation of the almighty God. The Holy Spirit is not a second blessing that comes some time after conversion. The Holy Spirit is Jesus Christ in spirit form. He is a third manifestation of the whole counsel of God. The Spirit is the third manifestation of the Trinity—the one God who is self-disclosed in three manifestations. He came in the Spirit in an upper room in Jerusalem on Pentecost just as Jesus came in the flesh and was laid in a manger in Bethlehem. We have seen God as Creator in chapter 4. We have seen God as Son in our discussion of Jesus. Now God is Holy Spirit indwelling and also empowering the people to live, to overcome, and to witness. Preaching of the Holy Spirit is a major aspect of preaching the whole counsel of God.

Third, the Holy Spirit empowers believers for ministry. Jesus made this clear in his statements just prior to his Ascension:

> And see, I am sending upon you what my Father promised; so stay here in the city until you have been clothed with power from on high (Luke 24:49, NRSV).

It is clear in Jesus' statements here that the Holy Spirit is a third manifestation of the presence of God among God's people. It is also clear that the Holy Spirit is an empowering agent that propels God's people to action. The Spirit's mission is not limited to making people "happy." The Spirit also makes them holy and whole. By some groups, the meaning of the infilling of the Holy Ghost is often limited to making people "happy" while in the worship setting. Too often this is also the theological meaning of the Holy Ghost in many churches. The people, then, experience what James Baldwin described when he said: "The transfiguring power of the Holy Ghost ended when the service ended, and salvation stopped at the church door."[18]

The Holy Spirit empowered the early Christians, and this empowerment was manifested in signs and wonders and healings and liberation. The transforming power of the Holy Spirit emboldened the early believers to confront and challenge the social injustices of their day.

To give an example: Peter and John had conducted a successful healing service in front of the temple (Acts 3). The authorities arrested them and ordered them to stop preaching Jesus (Acts 4). When they were released, they shared their humiliating experience with other believers, and this gave rise to a prayer meeting. They prayed:

> Sovereign Lord, who made the heaven and the earth, the sea, and everything in them, it is you who said by the Holy Spirit through our ancestor David, your servant:
> 'Why did the Gentiles rage,
>   and the peoples imagine vain
>   things?
> The kings of the earth took their
>   stand,
> and the rulers have gathered
>   together
> Against the Lord and against
>   his Messiah.'

For in this city, in fact, both Herod and Pontius Pilate, with the Gentiles and the peoples of Israel, gathered together against your holy servant Jesus. . . . And now, Lord, look at their threats, and grant to your servants to speak your word with all boldness. (Acts 4:24-29, NRSV).

The Holy Spirit not only empowered them to talk in tongues in the upper room on the day of Pentecost, but also emboldened them to talk against the evils of their day in the marketplace. We should preach the whole counsel of the Holy Spirit because of the Spirit's efficacy for empowering the people.

African American preachers attempting to preach the whole counsel of God have not given the same visibility to the Holy Spirit as has been given to God the Father and God the Son. The Holy Spirit, nevertheless, has been the empowering divine agent in the lives of African American believers. How else could they have endured and overcome the brutalities of slavery and oppression? How else could they have confronted and challenged the injustices of the modern Pharaohs, Herods, and Pontius Pilates?

The wind of the Holy Spirit is blowing all over the globe.

New groups are forming and making new interpretations and assertions about the Holy Spirit. However, in many instances, these interpretations are done in narrow and sectarian settings. More and more African Americans are being exposed to narrow and distorted views of the Holy Spirit. These views of the Holy Spirit must be corrected. African American academic theologians and preacher-theologians must go back to the hermeneutical workshops and examine afresh the meaning of the Holy Spirit in Scripture, in the Christian church throughout the centuries, and in the experience of African American believers. They must draw from the tradition of the Catholic church, the mainline Protestant denominations, and from the Pentecostals. All have something of value to say to each other.

We must have a theology that informs the preaching of the whole counsel of the Holy Spirit so that believers will be able to distinguish between the false alarms and the real "fire this time." We must have a practical theology of the Holy Spirit to undergird the pastor-theologians who Sunday after Sunday must address those with their backs against the wall. They need more than an inspiration to "shout." They need a transforming power to live.

Traditional preaching of the whole counsel of God among African Americans including Jesus and "The Fire Next Time" was the divine source of empowering the people. I will discuss this matter in the next chapter.

Chapter 6

Practical Preaching:
Empowering the People

We are a people with a story and a history of experiences; we must keep our story before us as a way of grounding and rooting ourselves. We must keep telling the stories that remind us of who we are. . . . The children in the ballet made it over the chasm because they told stories that reminded them of who they were.[1]

This excerpt from a sermon by Yvonne V. Delk makes an important point. African Americans, too, were empowered to overcome by hearing stories of who they were. They were human beings made in the image of God and they were the object of God's divine love and favor. Like the Israelites in Babylonian captivity of whom Yvonne Delk preached, they have been removed from their homeland by force, have survived, and have been empowered to overcome and to transcend the brutality of slavery and second-class citizenship because of divine intervention and divine help. The stories of redemption—the incidents of divine presence and divine deliverance—have been transmitted primarily through preaching and mainly in worship settings and contexts. These stories have also been perpetuated and transmitted in a variety of social contexts as well. The story of God's favor and African American survival has been and is being told in major social gatherings, such as the civil rights march on Washington on August 28, 1963, and in many lesser gatherings during the entire history of black presence in America. And, as Delk suggests, whenever two or three of "us" gathered together, it was and still is an occasion for telling the story of our sojourn and survival in America as a people.

Incidents of the stories of African American survival, transcendence, and overcoming have been intertwined with Israel's stories of oppression and deliverance of the Old Testament and with the New Testament redemption stories. Incidents of the African American stories have also been intertwined with the stories of Jesus of Nazareth, who came to set the captives free and to bring them into a confederation where his kingdom would come on earth as it is in heaven.

The biblical stories, combined with the stories of the African American experience, were told again and again in the worship contexts and anywhere that two or three might gather. The stories empowered the people. Cecelia N. Adkins, executive director of the Sunday school publishing board of the National Baptist Convention, USA, made a poignant point in her annual report in 1992 when she stated:

> The writing of those who have lived the black experience can offer strategies for survival in an unfriendly world where one must run twice as fast to get half as far, and work twice as hard to stay there once you have arrived.[2]

She was talking about the writings of African Americans who have lived the black experience. But her statement is a precise summary of the efficacy of practical preaching in the African American worship and social context. The preaching empowered an oppressed black people to run twice as fast even though they only covered half the distance of white Americans. This practical preaching also empowered an oppressed people to work twice as hard as white Americans to maintain any position that they might have achieved. The practical preaching empowered the people.

Context, Praxis, and Hermeneutics

The preaching context is multidimensional. It is spatial and universal; it is concrete and abstract; it is tangible and intangible. The preaching context has to do with the specific setting where preaching takes place, but it also takes into account the scriptural belief, history, experience, culture revelation, reason, and tradition of the preacher and hearers.

The spatial, concrete, and tangible context for preaching among African Americans is the worship centers and the places of social gatherings for empowerment in all kinds of forums. But the universal, abstract, and intangible context where African American preaching takes place is shaped by the religio-social condition of those who meet for worship and/or redemptive instructions and exhortations. The abstract context also includes the feelings and aspirations of a pilgrim people in the struggle for redemption in a nation where social justice has not been an experienced reality for all. In her sermon on "Singing the Lord's Song," Yvonne Delk reviewed the story of Israel's Babylonian captivity and discussed the challenge put to the Israelites by the Babylonians to "'Sing us one of the songs of Zion!'" (Psalm 137:3, NRSV):

> The Lord's song was created not only for Zion but for Babylon as well. We are called to sing God's song wherever people feel trapped, wherever they are hurting, oppressed, or struggling under overwhelming life-denying circumstances. . . . Those who have been in the valley of the shadow of death can sing the songs of Zion with power and meaning.[3]

When I speak of the context for practical African American preaching, I speak of the physical, social, and worship or liturgical setting, but I speak also of the nonmaterial spiritual-psychic-socio residue that permeates the life and existence of those who stand at moments in human history with their backs against the wall. This aspect of the context evolves out of a situation where people lack adequate access to food, housing, education, health care, and social and cultural enrichment. This context exists for a people whose survival has always been at stake.

This aspect of the African American context for preaching and practical theology is shaped by praxis. Praxis is not synonymous with practice. Praxis has to do with the critical correlation or relationship between theory and practice. The correlation is dialectical. This means that theory and practice engage each other and are formed and revised by each other. The dialectical process is operative when theory negates practice and practice seems to negate theory. However, this process opens up new theoretical and practical possibilities, and the process continues.

Praxis involves all of the social and cultural thoughts and

practices of persons involved in social and cultural interaction upon each other and upon themselves. Praxis has to do with the results of the actions of a person upon himself or herself and others in a group. It also has to do with the results of the action of one group upon another group in a particular community or society. Praxis is the milieu out of which mores, practices, and institutions are formulated. It is a dynamic process in all communities and societies.

The preaching of African Americans is shaped by the material and nonmaterial context, and the context is directly influenced by the indigenous praxis of African Americans—the theory and practices that they are experiencing and passing through at a particular time and their whole experience in America. The African American praxis is a praxis undergirded with a redemption motif. This redemption motif leads to the structuring of a practical theology—an applied theology—that empowers the African American people to become actively involved with God in the redemptive acts of binding up the wounds of those who are bruised from oppression, assisting them to become involved in resistance and empowering them in ridding the "Jericho roads" of the robbers who cause harm and injury to the travelers. The main robber on the "Jericho roads" in America today is an inhumane national and international economic system. This practical theology out of praxis undergirds and affirms persons and humanity in the social context of their existence. It affirms the ontology—the personal being—of the oppressed. It gives meaning to being in a state of human-caused nonbeing.

Preachers who have sat where the people sat in struggle and pain appeared on the scene with an empowering word, and the people shouted:

How beautiful upon the
      mountains
   are the feet of the messenger
      who announces peace,
who brings good news,
      who announces salvation,
      who says to Zion, "Your God
reigns."
            —Isaiah 52:7 (NRSV)

Then the preachers in that context, out of an African American praxis, led the singing of Zion songs with power and meaning. This practical preaching required a hermeneutical approach, which is also circumscribed by the African American praxis. While hermeneutics has a universal definition—meaning a theory of interpretation—it loses much of its universality as a tool of interpretation when it is applied in the African American context. For example, it is difficult to use the same methodology of interpretation of the Scripture, experience, and meaning of the ontology of the oppressors in the African American context. The methodology of hermeneutics for African Americans was derived from the African American praxis. And it is precisely this African American hermeneutic that has informed a practical theology, which informed African American preaching, which in turn empowered an oppressed people. It strengthened their ontological self-understanding as persons made in the image of God. People were empowered to identify with the mysterious and the transcendence beyond the logical and the practical.

Ella Pearson Mitchell brought a new hermeneutical approach to her sermon "The Welcome Table." The text was John 13:4-5, 12-17, 20, the story of the Lord's Supper and Jesus' washing of the feet of his disciples.[4] Mitchell's primary hermeneutical approach in this sermon was not to focus on the theological meaning of the Lord's Supper and its salvific and sacramental value, not that this aspect is unimportant to African Americans. Mitchell, however, elected to focus on the interpretation of that aspect of the story that dealt with Jesus' becoming a servant to his disciples.

I believe that Mitchell's focus upon this aspect of the story was a conscious and a deliberate attempt to preach out of praxis. She broke away from the traditional hermeneutical approach to this text.

Three points are made clear to me in this aspect of the sermon. One, Jesus bound the group into a kind of confederation and challenged them to become a servant community. This way, they could enjoy the abundant life. Ella put these words in the mouth of Jesus:

"Frankly, if you know what I'm talking about, you'll be most happy and blessed to actually do this service for others. This is no terrible, degrading chore; it is the way abundant living becomes a reality for your life."[5]

This is a new way of interpreting this facet of the story from an African American practical preaching perspective.

Second, Mitchell continued her interpretation of the story by pointing out that, while some surrounded the Lord's Supper in mystical piety and ceremonious splendor, she found in the writing of Luke and John that, even at the Lord's Table, Jesus insisted on relating to the real needs and rights of people. "Our Lord has no place for a sanctity separated from service," she declared.[6]

Third, Mitchell noted that the welcome table is an inclusive table. This is always an important message when preached among a people who have and are experiencing systematic exclusion in too many forums of life.

The African American preaching context is material and non-material. It includes the place of gathering in church and in the community. It also includes the total existence of a people evolving out of the African American praxis. The context provides the forum for the judicial hermeneutical approach, which interprets the meaning of God and redemption for the hearers so that they are empowered.

Preaching Redemption

The central theme of African American preaching that has made it so efficacious and empowering has been the redemption motif—what God has done, is doing, and will do in the life and history of people on the underside of life. This idea of God as Redeemer who is active in human history permeates African American preaching. In a sermonic lecture, the Reverend Samuel Austin declared:

> Throughout sacred history the *action* of God is being applied to each generation. Within the context of Salvation history the Black Church discovers more fully how God can be known by what he *does*. In Exodus He's a God of liberation. In Joshua He's a God of righteous warfare.... In Ezekiel He's a God of hope to a hopeless people. In Daniel He's a God of deliverance (Emphasis added).[7]

The point is that God is the Redeemer who is known through his action and what he *does* in human history. It is this preaching that gives great hope to persons in need of liberation and deliverance. This preaching of redemption is apparent everywhere in the African American community.

The story is told of a boy who had learned how to do wood carving. He made a little boat and took it down to the stream near his home. Playing with the boat in the water, the boy lost it as it got away from him and was carried down the stream. The boat was lost and the little boy was unable to find it. Several weeks later, the boy was walking down the street in his hometown. Passing an antique shop and seeing what he was sure to be his boat, he went in and assured the proprietor that the boat was his. The proprietor said he had secured the boat from an unknown person, but if the boy really made the boat and really wanted it back, he would have to purchase it for the sum of two dollars. The boy purchased the boat. Then the boy, while walking down the street with joy and exuberance, began to talk to his boat. "Little boat, you're mine. You're mine twice; you're mine because I made you and you're mine because I bought you."[8]

This was the story of redemption, the idea of self-worth and self-esteem that was transmitted to the people over and over again through practical preaching. It was the story of God's love for his people. African Americans were assured that God made them and God bought them. This was an empowering story.

Dr. T. J. Jemison, president of the National Baptist Convention, USA, lifted up this empowering redemption theme in his tenth annual address, during the 112th annual session in Atlanta on September 10, 1992. At one point, he said ". . . We have not reached the promised land, but we are no longer in the wilderness." At another point, he declared, "The National Baptist Convention, U.S.A., Inc. will take us into the twenty-first century unbowed and unafraid, trusting in God as we have done for the past 112 years."[9]

In these preached lines and stories, the listeners identified with the characters; thus, the God of the people of the Exodus was also their God. The delegates were assured that the God who brought their parents out of the wilderness would bring them into the promised land. The message or sermon of the African American preacher was also the message or sermon of the people. It was the audible expression of their faith, their aspiration, and their hope.

One white professor of preaching, Fred B. Craddock, who recognized this phenomena in the black preaching and worship tradition, wrote:

> [Black] congregations are able to recognize the sermon as their own much more than in those churches in which the sermon is the minister's own possession, before which the congregation sits silently waiting to see what the preacher has brought to them today.

To say that in many black churches the sermon is recognized as their own is to say that they are familiar with it.[10]

The Preaching Style

What are some of the unique identifying features of African American practical preaching that conveyed the redemption theme in such a positive way that the preaching empowered the people? The response to this question leads to the discussion of the matter of style. However, this book does not focus on the development of a meaningful preaching style. It presents excerpts from the rich traditional preaching style or styles in the African American church.

Style is the vehicle that conveys the message of eternal salvation and earthly deliverance in the usual context of worship of a people conditioned by a stride toward freedom in their particular time and place, usually by the preacher. Style is the way in which manner, method, word, tone, and feeling are appropriated in African American preaching. J. Alfred Smith put it this way:

> Style is the manner in which a speaker uses language in expressing thought. . . . Style is the uniqueness of the preacher's way of communication. Style is the mirror of the thought and thought forms of the preacher. The personality, natural mental gifts, training, and cultural tastes are components which constitute style.[11]

Style is a part of the immaterial context of African American preaching, since the preacher is a part of the preaching context as well as the audience. The dialogical symphony between the preacher and the audience form the grand preaching context.

Personal style and variation in individual style are distinguishing features in African American preaching.

Rhetoric, repetition, rhythm, rest, spontaneity, tone, chant, cadence, melody, drama, and epic are distinguishing elements in the African American preaching style.[12] Of course, not all of these elements are used in each sermon. The audience context has great influence on the preacher context. The word *rhetoric* can have a negative connotation if it is used to mean the skillful and crafty manipulation of language in order to hold attention, to induce, and to persuade persons for the sole purpose of advancing the personal cause of the speaker.

In an article titled "The Rhetoric of Malcolm X," John Illo argued:

> In a nation of images without substance, of rehearsed emotions, in a politic of consensus, where platitude replaces belief or belief is fashioned by consensus, genuine rhetoric, like authentic prose, must be rare. For rhetoric, like any verbal art, is correlative with a pristine idea of reason and justice . . . .[13]

If rhetoric is merely rehearsed emotions used in order to evoke consensus, irrespective of truth and value, this is not genuine rhetoric. Rhetoric in African American preaching is genuine. It is a nonmaterial cultural survival of the African tradition. It is the natural way of being responsive to the divine mandate of interpretation and proclamation. It is an elucidation of faith and reason flowing out of the honesty of the heart, mind, and soul. Most of the early African American preachers had little or no formal education and even less training in rhetoric. However, along with developing charisma, they also developed an unusual ability to preach rhetorically, using language to make statements and to ask questions, to make assertions and to imply conclusions, emoting reason, faith, and feelings.

In "Spiritual Counsel in Carnal Crises," Sandy Ray asserted that preachers ought to have a personal story of an encounter with God and that they ought to include their personal stories in their preaching. To make that point, Ray used the rhetorical method as follows: "I wonder if Paul ever related his experience to the priesthood? I often wonder if he ever got a chance to tell his Damascus road experience to the priesthood?"[14]

It is not by mistake that Ray raised the question twice. This was deliberate. Between the first and second stating of the question, there was rest—pause—before the repetition. The rest was intentional; it gave the audience time to think, to feel, and to respond with, "Yes," "That's right," or "Amen." However, all audience responses and feedback are not audible. There are other affirmations of the heart that may or may not be observable to onlookers. It might be a feeling heard and understood by a community of soul sisters and brothers.

After profoundly raising the question and observing the rest and repetition involving the audience, which is characteristic of good African American preaching, Ray responded to the rhetorical question and made an assertion: "Every time he [Paul] got in a close place, he would relate the Damascus road experience."[15] The response of the audience was verbal and thunderous. Ray continued:

> And whenever there were situations in which he was involved that he couldn't quite explain what was happening to him, he would say, "When I was on the road to Damascus . . ." And whenever he told this story, it had something very, very thrilling to do with the life of people. Might I just drop here, I think preachers ought to tell this experience. When we are talking about firstly, and secondly, and thirdly, and in the first place, and in the second place, I think every once in a while we ought to tell about our Damascus road.[16]

This was good rhetoric, rest, repetition, and feedback characteristic of good African American preaching. Spontaneity is another element in the African American preaching style. The preceding paragraph was not included in the original manuscript. As a master preacher, Ray spontaneously added that section to the sermon and at the same time maintained coherence, continuity, and integrity. When asked about these insertions into the preached sermons that were not found in the circulated manuscript, Ray responded: "I prepare my sermons like a newscaster prepares the news report. I use all of the information available at that time, but often, when the newscaster gets on the set, some 'late-breaking' news always comes in over the wires." So, like a newscaster, Ray spontaneously inserted "late-breaking" divine announcements into his prepared manuscript. This led Henry Mitchell to rightly conclude that sermons "in the Black tradition, were preached and *heard*, not written to be read."[17]

The African American's sermon is not prepared, like a meal, frozen and then thawed in the microwave of the worship setting for serving. The sermonic meal is always in preparation even while being served. There is freedom of expression in the pulpit. There is plenty of room for the intervention of the Holy Spirit. This ingenuity of including spontaneity and adding rhetoric and rest in a rhythmic fashion in the preached sermon gives it a vitality that not only inspires but also invigorates and empowers the listeners.

Other powerful and pronounced elements in African American preaching include tone or melody—the African nonmaterial cultural survival that gives the sermon a kind of singing quality. That tone—"tuning up"—or melodic quantity in African American preaching gives the sermon a congregational dimension. It is a type of "tuning" that gets the congregation involved, and the sermon is no longer the presentation of the preacher. It is the song of the congregation, and the preacher is the soloist or the lead singer. The sermon is responsorial—the preacher assumes the lead part and the congregation responds in a variety of ways—audibly, with bodily movements, or simply by countenance affirmation. Thus, we have a congregational preaching choir. The venerable Caesar Clark is the epitome of the tonal and melodic African American preacher today.

Another highlighting element in preaching that electrifies and empowers the mass African American congregations is chanting or cadence. This is not too different from tone and melody, except that chanting and cadence in African American preaching has to do with intentional timing in the use of words, phrases, and sentences. The sermons of Sandy Ray were not so much tonal and melodic as those of Caesar Clark, but Ray's sermons were replete with chanting and cadence. In "Spiritual Counsel," Ray had Paul addressing the captains and the pilots on the apparently ill-fated ship in Acts 27:13-44:

> "The angel of the Lord, (rest and audience response)
> whose I am and whom I serve,
> stood by me this night.

While thunders were rolling,
while lightnings were flashing,
while winds were blowing,
the angel of the Lord,
whose I am and whom I serve,
stood by me this night.
Be of good cheer."
Sounds just like a preacher.
"Everything's going to be all right."
Winds are blowing,
ship leaking,
storm raging,
but the preacher says,
"Everything is going to be all right."[18]

Martin Luther King Jr. was also known for the use of cadence in his preaching. Louis Lomax noted that when King arrived at a church in an Alabama town on Friday, December 6, 1955, the church had been packed with people since five o'clock that afternoon, and now three thousand people were standing outside waiting to hear what turned out to be the call for an all-out bus boycott in Montgomery, Alabama. After a list of other speakers, King approached the rostrum and began his empowering and enabling speech this way:

King (K): "There comes a time when people get tired."
Audience (A): "Yes, Lord."
(K): "We are here this evening to say to those who have mistreated us for so long that we are tired—"
(A): "Help him, Jesus!"
(K): "—we are tired of being segregated and humiliated."
(A): "Amen."
(K): ". . . tired! . . . did you hear me when I said 'tired'?"
(A): "Yes, Lord!"[19]

People were motivated and empowered by that sermon. They acted and transformed an oppressive social system.

Remember, good African American preaching is preached and heard, not written to be read. And the reader would have to hear the preaching of the successors to the preaching tradition of Ray and King in order to appreciate the value in the chant and the cadence, the timing and the rests that are imbedded in this motivating and empowering kind of preaching.

Familiar epics in the African American tradition/religion are regularly employed as salient elements in preaching. Epics are citations, roll calling, lines, brief sayings, narratives, and stories regularly employed in preaching to drive home a point or to clinch the theological truth of God's action in creation or in human history and/or God's eschatological promises. These epics begin with familiar, condensed Bible stories, or roll calling, such as the roll call of the hall of faith found in Hebrews 11. It could be Psalm 23, Psalm 121, or Isaiah 53:5: "He was wounded for our transgressions . . . ," or Luke 4:18: "The Spirit of the Lord is upon me . . ." (NRSV). Listeners identify with the redemption stories of the hall of faith and others, and they are empowered to hold on and to move forward.

These and other biblical epics tend to spontaneously creep into the sermon, although the preacher has used a totally different text as the foundation. In "Spiritual Counsel," Ray had Paul warning the crew, passengers, and prisoners on the ship:

> There is a competent pilot on board.
> He is the "Lily of the Valley," . . . .
> He is the "Rose of Sharon," . . . .
> He is the "Stone cut out of
> mountains without hands," . . . .
> He is a "battle ax," . . . .
> He is the "Rock of Ages," . . . .
> He is Wonderful, Counselor, Everlasting Father,
> Mighty God, and Prince of Peace.[20]

Epics also include nonbiblical sayings. Lines from the hymns, spirituals, and gospel songs were also regularly employed in African American preaching. For example: "I don't believe he brought me this far to leave me." Many preachers regularly end their sermons with such lines or those from some other familiar source. Others regularly end their sermons with familiar biblical passages.

The importance of climax is also special in African American preaching. Generally, the seasoned preachers would begin the sermon in a moderate conversational voice and gradually intensify the tempo, climaxing in a crescendo. However, many great African American sermons do not follow this pattern. While climax—or making the main point on a profound note with gusto—is present in the preacher context, many good African American sermons have several high points and several low points and still make the primary point at the end. Thus, preachers and people might say that he or she "really had a good climax." Climax generally means ending, "how you bring it home—make the major salvific point." But I will point out in chapter 7 that climax in good African American preaching is often internal as well as at the end.

Empowering the People

African American preaching is a weekly therapeutic injection to patients who have been victimized by racism and oppression, to give them the vitality to participate in their healing—in their redemption. The practical theology energizing the sermon is transmitted to the people, energizing them to swim against the tide, to struggle against the odds, to creatively engage in the redemptive movement. The theological interpretation gives essence to the message. The dynamic proclamation gives empowerment to the people.

It is the preaching that gives them directions for family and communal development and for engaging in direct confrontation with a hostile secular world. African American preaching is never addressed "To whom it may concern." It is always directed to the specific sisters and brothers in their social context of existence. This preaching not only has a specific address, it also gives or implies specific directions for action—for involvement in the divine plan of redemption.

What James Earl Massey said about sermons in general is characteristic of traditional good African American sermons: "The sermon design is therefore ordered for the sake of an experience; it is planned to make a hearing a 'happening'."[21] There has always been great interest in right meaning and correct belief, but the African American sermon has also been preoccupied with or planned to elicit right action. The preaching helps the people to discern the times and to act with God in improving the lot of the dispossessed. The extraordinary power of the gospel keeps alive a redemptive hope and gives meaning to the confederation—communal cohesiveness—of a fragmented people.

In a sermon titled "Women for Such a Time as This," Martha Jean Simmons used the text Esther 4:14. She related the story of Esther becoming the queen to Ahasuerus, King of Persia. Being a Hebrew, she had been instructed by her uncle Mordecai to speak to the king on the matter of relief for the oppressed Hebrews. Simmons said that, after some apprehension, Esther wrote a letter to her uncle:

> Dear Uncle Mordecai, I got your message. . . . Uncle, I know you're right. . . . I was made queen for a reason. So, soon and very soon I'm going to see the King and "if I perish, I perish."[22]

Because of the action of Esther, deliverance came to the oppressed Hebrews. Simmons concluded: "You see, when oppressed people find themselves in distress, it's not because God is dead. The people just need to rise up and do something for themselves and God will do the rest."[23] Simmons was preaching in the African American tradition for a verdict. She intended to make a hearing a happening among the listeners.

The preaching in African American tradition moved the hearers from orthodoxy to orthopraxis. The hearers were moved from the concern for right doctrine—orthodoxy—to become involved in right action—orthopraxis. Right thought was to be actualized into right action. The question went beyond "What can I know?" to "What must I do?" The answer was always given or implied in the sermons: "You must become involved in the mission of liberation and confederation wherever you are. You are to become involved in interpreting situations and becoming involved with God in challenging distortions and solving problems and correcting errors." The sermons empowered the people for getting through the world.

The preaching was founded in practical theology and practical theology is theology in action. It moves beyond pious platitudes to become involved in the struggle for joy and fulfillment in the real-life situation of the people.

In "Theology on Our Feet," Thomas Groome argued that theology must be more than for our heads; it must be theology on our feet; it must be both practical and political. We must believe, he argued, that God sets us free both personally and politically, and therefore the task of Christian theology goes beyond the interpretation of the world; it must empower the Christians to become involved in changing the world.[24] This was precisely the practical theological premise of African American preacher-theologians. It was they who transmitted this truth to the people. The sermons pointed always to God's promise, God's faithfulness, and a better tomorrow that is ordained by God.

Incidents of the empowerment of African American people to engage in struggles to change a world that was always hostile toward them include the rebellions over the centuries of their sojourn in America. Through preaching, they were impelled and sustained in the organization of emancipation and freedom movements. They organized churches, educational institutions, labor unions, political groups, burial societies, hospitals, insurance companies, newspapers, banks, and businesses of every sort. They were empowered to form social and liberation organizations, including the National Association for the Advancement of Colored People (NAACP), the Congress of Racial Equality (CORE), the Southern Christian Leadership Conference (SCLC), the Student Non-Violent Coordinating Committee (SNCC), and many other like organizations, including black caucuses in most major white religious denominations with an African American constituency.

African American preachers preached into being the Montgomery bus boycott and the civil rights movement. The masses of African American folk in Montgomery, Alabama, got the word of inspiration to participate in the Montgomery bus boycott not through the mass media, but rather through the preaching pulpits in 1955. African American preachers also preached into being the 1963 march on Washington, and at that rally, King preached many African Americans and their white friends into recommitting themselves to returning to their cities, towns, and hamlets to continue the struggle to change the racist system in America.

"Go Back and Wait!" is the title of a sermon preached by the Reverend Shirley Virginia Knight Budd. The text was Acts 1:4-5, 12.[25] This was the story of Jesus after the Resurrection and before the Ascension, instructing his disciples to return to Jerusalem and wait for the promise of the Father, which would empower them for ministry. Biblical texts are often interpreted with double meaning in African American preaching. Budd pointed out that people often feel spiritually bankrupt, and, often, turning to familiar hymns and even to prayer do not always seem to help. She confessed that she recently had such an experience, then she opened her Bible to Acts 1:4-5, 12 and got the message "Go back and wait!"

The idea of going back to Jerusalem in the text, she said, was because "the name 'Zion' . . . became the title for Jerusalem as a whole in its quality as a holy city." And "the sanctity of Zion is accounted for by the fact that it was for many years the abiding place of the Ark and was celebrated as such by David."[26] She said that, although Jerusalem had many times been besieged and had suffered many grievous famines, there is no record of the inhabitants ever lacking water. Jerusalem was also fortified and thus a city of widest influence.

Budd concluded that the disciples "had been empowered to bring others to Christ by the outpouring of the Holy Ghost." For the listeners, this sermon would have a double meaning. It meant that the waiting in Jerusalem and the outpouring of the Holy Ghost empowered the disciples to become engaged in evangelism. The sermon also spoke to the social context of the existence of the listeners. They could "go back and wait" because, like the city of Jerusalem, they too had been besieged, cut off from economic resources, and had suffered grievously, but the water of the Spirit of God flowed from Zion and kept the people alive and viable. The sermon was a sermon of empowerment for ministry and for social action.

In that "I Have a Dream" speech, King urged the listeners to "go back to Mississippi, go back to Alabama, go back to South Carolina, go back to Georgia, go back to Louisiana, go back to the slums and ghettos of our northern cities, knowing that somehow this situation can and will be changed."[27]

This was a clear summons to action. It was theologically grounded in the belief that God had ordained ultimate victory. The audience present and those viewing and listening via electronic media were empowered to go back to their particular locales and to participate in God's preordained plan of this-worldly redemption.

This speech—sermon—was also very celebrative in style and context. The audience was caught up in the celebration. In the following chapter, I will discuss preaching and celebration.

Chapter 7

Preaching and Celebration

Then the prophet Miriam, Aaron's sister, took a tambourine in her hand; and all the women went out after her with tambourines and with dancing. And Miriam sang to them: "Sing to the Lord, for he has triumphed gloriously; horse and rider he has thrown into the sea" (Exodus 15: 20-21, NRSV).

Biblical Celebrations

Celebration permeated the tradition of the Israelites. In the text quoted above, Miriam implored the women to join the men in a celebrative expression and song, which began in Exodus 15:1. In fact, Miriam led the women to repeat the first four lines of the victory song. From the words, it is very clear why the celebration was in order. "The Lord has triumphed gloriously." The Lord had intervened in human history and redeemed them by drowning their enemies, horses and riders, in the Red Sea. In a very tangible way, the presence of God had been manifested in their earthly and oppressive situation.

Another incident of celebration in worship in the Old Testament was when David discovered that the Lord had blessed the house of Obed-edom, a Gentile, because he kept there the Ark of the Covenant.

> David went and brought up the ark of God up from the house of Obed-edom to the city of David with rejoicing. . . . David danced before the Lord with all his might. . . . So David and all the house of Israel brought up the ark of the Lord with shouting, and with the sound of the trumpet (2 Samuel 6:12-15, NRSV).

In the New Testament, the early church had its genesis in a preaching-celebrative context. It was the day of Pentecost; the promise of the outpouring of the Holy Spirit had now been fulfilled among the original disciples and other believers. This divine outpouring and the ecstatic response of praise and worship of the 120 persons who had experienced the infilling caused inquisitive query among the unsuspecting observers. They were amazed and perplexed, asking one another "what is the meaning of this?" Some shrugged off the event by saying, "They are filled with new wine" (Acts 2:13, NRSV).

This provided the opportunity for preaching, and in this first unscheduled worship and sermon of the early church, Peter attempted to preach the whole counsel of God. He preached the sovereignty, plan, promise, and faithfulness of God. He preached Jesus, "this man handed over to you according to the *definite plan* and foreknowledge of God, you crucified and killed by the hands of those outside the law" (Acts 2:23, NRSV, emphasis added). He preached the ministries—deeds, wonders, and signs—of Jesus of Nazareth. He preached the Crucifixion and the Resurrection. He preached "The Fire Next Time"—the fulfilled promise of the outpouring of the Holy Spirit. The preaching itself was so celebrative of the truths that were communicated that the listeners cried out, "Brothers, what should we do?" (Acts 2:37, NRSV).

Peter's celebrative preaching of the whole counsel motivated and empowered the people to do something. The celebration of the whole counsel of God in the preaching made a hearing a happening. About three thousand of those who heard this message repented and were baptized and were added to the new fellowship of believers. They became students of the apostles' teachings, engaged in fellowship, festive meals, prayer, and other worship experiences.

I have had the opportunity to travel to the African continent twice, visiting four countries. By this experience and by study and observation, I have concluded that celebration—the joyful and ecstatic expressions in worship and other social settings—is a major element in the African culture.

African American Worship Celebrations

Celebration in African American worship settings is greatly influenced, I believe, by their understanding of worship and celebration in the Bible. But, more particularly, the expressive glorification and enjoyment in African American worship is a nonmaterial African cultural survival.

The term "celebration" has several definitions and connotations. The term is used many times to mean the performance of a public religious ceremony or some sacred rite, such as celebrating Holy Communion, the Mass, or a marriage. Or it could mean the celebration of a holy or special day. Celebration in this case goes beyond the solemnization or officiating during a religious liturgy, rite, or ceremony. Here celebration means joyful, ecstatic, enthusiastic, and glorious expressions in mass African American worship and preaching. This celebration evokes a sense of enjoyment and transcendence among the people. Celebration is adoration and edification; it is vitality in thanksgiving; it is reverence in expressions. This celebrative element in worship and preaching is creative, artistic, empowering, and redemptive.

Celebration in African American worship is not to be confused with simple or rehearsed emotionalism. This celebration might be expressed emotionally, but the emotion is not the end. It is one form of the means by which joy and ecstasy and glory and praise are uttered to God out of the overflow of gratitude of persons who are experiencing the full reality of being.

Like Moses, Miriam, and the Israelites, African Americans celebrate their remembrance of God's redemptive acts with their voices and with their whole being. Like David, they unashamedly dance before the Lord as an expression of gratitude and highest praise.

E. Franklin Frazier discussed the shout songs that flourished among the African Americans on the Sea Islands off the coast of South Carolina and Georgia. These shout songs, Frazier said, were so named because they were and "are still sung while the Negro worshipers are engaged in what might be called a holy dance." He continued that this form of expression was an example of a primitive and elemental expression of religion among the Negroes. It provided, he said, a good illustration of the contention advanced by R. R. Marett that "primitive man 'does not preach his religion, but dances it instead.'"[1]

What Frazier was implying about three decades ago was that the Negro religious practices on those Sea Islands was a primitive form of religious worship. The idea of "primitive" here suggests that as the Negroes would be more exposed to the "refined and civilized" Euro-American style of worship, these "primitive" practices would vanish. Some African American preachers were also influenced by this misconception.

Bishop Daniel A. Payne, an African American bishop who pastored the Bethel A.M.E. Church near Baltimore in 1878, had this to say as he observed a worship service replete with celebration:

> After the sermon they formed a ring, and, with coats off, sang, clapped their hands, and stamped their feet in a most ridiculous and heathenish way. I requested the pastor to go and stop their dancing. . . . To the most thoughtful and intelligent, I usually succeeded in making the "Band" disgusting; but by the ignorant masses . . . it was regarded as the essence of religion. . . . Someone has even called it a "Voodoo dance."[2]

In 1964 Joseph R. Washington Jr., who had gone through the Euro-American institution of higher learning and who had accepted the Euro-American worship style as normative, wrote *Black Religion: The Negro and Christianity in the United States.* Washington, using the white church worship style as normative, said that the African American churches were amusement centers where people went to be entertained.[3] Washington suggested that these ill-contrived worship expressions were held among African American people with little or no education and were led by pastors from the same background.

Well, if the late E. Franklin Frazier or Joseph Washington could visit a worship service at the Bethel A.M.E. Church or the Mt. Lebanon Baptist Church in Baltimore today, either might draw the same conclusion that Bishop Payne articulated a century ago. However, not only these, but other Methodist and Baptist and other mainline African American churches around the nation are tending to be more vocal in expressions, with hand clapping and "dancing" as ongoing entities in their worship settings.

What of these overt and other expressions in worship today that transcend educational and social background and are not limited to the Pentecostal or holiness groups? This phenomenon has moved into churches across intellectual and denominational lines. In many learned congregations where pastor and people are professionals and paraprofessionals with advanced degrees, some with the terminal degrees, the tide of overt celebration is flooding the church. Certainly not all people in all churches engage in overt joyful and ecstatic expressions in worship. This is not to be interpreted, however, that quietness means the absence of spiritual involvement. Recently in a highly "charged" worship setting, I sat next to a person who generally does not celebrate in an audible fashion. But by sitting next to her I could hear her quiet "amens" and observe her frequent physical motions of affirmation. She was deeply involved in the joyful and glorious celebration.

Is this rising tide of expressive celebration all "good"? Is it all "bad"? Of course, "good" and "bad" are relative terms. These are relative questions. Certainly it is "bad" or negative when the celebration becomes contrived emotionalism, when the experience provides more heat than light and when people are led to whoop and holler but go away not helped and healed and empowered to engage meaningfully in living for self and for others. The celebration is useless when there is no understood theological foundation for the celebration.

Four realities should be acknowledged. One, expressive celebration in the African American churches is returning and pervasive. Two, this phenomenon is going to go with us into the twenty-first century. Three, some form of celebration has always been an element in African American worship tradition. In the early days of African American religious worship, joyful and ecstatic expressions were regularly employed in the services. At points along the way, white people and some black people convinced some of the African American churches, denominations, and leaders that this form of behavior was primitive and nonsense and unacceptable as normative. This inhibited joyful expressions in certain churches. But the fire of joyful and glorious ecstasy was never completely extinguished. It was, from time to time, smoldering, only to burst out into open flames again and again. And it is burning like a wildfire across this nation today. A fourth reality that should be acknowledged is that there is a need for study and theological reflection of this phenomenon of celebration in African American worship.

There is a biblical foundation for celebration, as we have discovered through Moses, Miriam, David, and the early church. Academic theologians and preacher-theologians must seriously reflect upon this wave of joyful and ecstatic expression in worship and find means of incorporating these reflections in the preaching, teaching, and worship of the church. This must be done so that celebration will not become an end in itself and just a "sideshow." Theology must inform celebration, and celebration ought to have a sound theological foundation.

A Theology of Celebration

While celebration in this book means the joyful, ecstatic, enthusiastic, and glorious expression in religious worship, we need to move toward the development of a theology of celebration. A theology of celebration is the doctrinal belief in the African American religious community that God is the author of celebration. God ordained celebration. God expects celebration among his people, and God honors celebration. God instructed Moses to bring the people into a place chosen by God. There they would engage in religious rites and ceremonies of burnt offerings and sacrifices and tithes. But God further instructed them:

> You shall *rejoice* before the LORD your God, you together with your sons and your daughters, your male and female slaves, and the Levites who reside in your towns . . . (Deuteronomy 12:12, NRSV, emphasis added).

This call to rejoicing, if properly interpreted by the Israelites, was manifested in their celebrations as recorded in the Psalms and elsewhere. One example:

Praise the LORD!
Sing to the LORD a new song,
    his praise in the assembly of
        the faithful.
Let Israel be glad in its Maker;
    let the children of Zion rejoice

in their king.
Let them praise his name with
    dancing,
making melody to him with
    tambourine and lyre.
For the LORD takes pleasure in
    his people.
    —Psalm 149:1-4 (NRSV)

The promise of Jesus is also: "Where two or three are gathered in my name, I am there among them" (Matthew 18:20, NRSV). The Bible clearly shows that the Lord ordained, expects, and honors joyful worship celebrations. It is from these biblical understandings and assertions that we frame our theological conclusion. It is out of this practical theological belief that this enthusiastic celebration ought to continue today.

Any aspect of worship can become distorted and polluted, so the African American custodians and transmitters of this pristine and genuine biblical, celebrative tradition in worship must be vigilant and critical. They must see that only the very best, wholesome, and empowering aspect of this tradition is passed on to succeeding generations. We must not shout just to be shouting or because it is fashionable in the 1990s. James Baldwin vividly reminded us of his church experience of gross celebration. He discovered that what he experienced as the transforming power of the Holy Ghost while in church worship often ended when the service ended, and salvation seemed to have stopped at the church's door. Authentic African American celebration embodies spiritual transcendence and spiritual and social empowerment.

I am using the terms "celebrate" and "shout" interchangeably. In *Why Black People Tend to Shout*, Ralph Wiley made this declaration:

> Black people tend to shout in churches, movie theaters, and anywhere else they feel the need to shout, because when joy, pain, anger, confusion and frustration, ego and thought, mix it up, the way they do inside black people, the uproar is too big to hold inside. The feeling must be aired.[4]

Wiley concluded that black folk shout because of pent-up

frustrations, disappointments, and anxieties. He was correct. These anxieties are often multiplied by human-caused social, political, and economic deprivation. Wiley helped us to understand, too, that black folk's shouts are not limited to the church. Black folk might shout anywhere.

There is another compelling reason, however, why black folk tend to shout. They shout in responsiveness to God for realized earthly salvation from woes. It is a celebration of liberation. They shout for the same reason that Moses and Miriam and David and the early disciples shouted—earthly deliverances *and* eternal salvation. Wiley addressed this salvific meaning of shout in the black tradition in the following statement:

> Black people tend to shout because nothing has come close to making those of the African diaspora less determined, or less artistic, or less inventive, or less adaptable, or less productive, or less wise, or less creative, or less quite stupendously gorgeous.[5]

He continued his argument that black people shout because nothing can stop the impulse of new meaning in the life of each succeeding generation. For African Americans who are active in the church and for the nonchurched who are greatly influenced by the black church tradition, it is the almighty God who has kept them determined, artistic, inventive, adaptable, productive, wise, creative, and stupendously gorgeous—"Black and Beautiful." Thus, they tend to shout; in church they celebrate these mighty acts and the ever presence of God. They celebrate the God who is Creator, who takes off the wheels of the chariots of the oppressors, and who is bringing about liberty and justice for all.

In gratefulness for these manifold blessings, African Americans tend to shout; they celebrate with the abiding conviction that "if I don't praise him, the rock's gonna cry out."[6] Celebration is an integral, authentic, and wholesome aspect of worship in the mass African American churches and communities. The preaching is central in the celebration.

The Sermon as Celebration

In African American preaching, the preacher always came with a revelation. This revelation was always communicated with an inspiration and with a celebration. It was a matter of glorifying God and involving the hearers. The sermon was the testimony of both the scriptural characters and of the preacher. Gloria Gerald preached the story of the woman who met Jesus at the well in Samaria. She put these words in the mouth of the unnamed woman:

> As I turned away from the well that blistering afternoon, I decided that I would not tell anyone about my experience— who would believe me anyway? Walking back home, I meditated over what had happened. Suddenly my pace increased, . . . and I started running because something within was compelling me. And I knew that I could not keep it to myself—*I had to tell somebody!* . . . By the time I reached the temple, practically everyone in the city had gathered around me. . . . after all, I was a "woman of ill repute." I was despised and rejected. . . . but I did know that I could not keep it to myself—*I had to tell somebody!*[7]

Here was a woman who had a special experience with Jesus; to testify of that experience was a compelling burden bursting out of her soul. The preacher in the African American church is not just an impartial media journalist who reports what has happened between God and God's people in human history as recorded in Scripture. The preacher is one who has also experienced what those in the stories experienced, and therefore the preacher is both reporter and witness of the story being related. Gerald's sermon moved from a report that it happened at the well in Sychar two thousand years ago to a testimony that "I experienced an encounter" and "We, too, have experienced transforming encounters with Jesus Christ in our life situations."

The preacher and the people are in a celebrative mode because the testimonies of the participants in the story also become their testimonies. The preacher is the ecstatic reporter, characteristic of the peddlers of the Mid-Atlantic cities of the 1940s through the 1970s who sold their goods in the streets.

When I came to Baltimore from South Carolina in 1948, one of the exciting sights in the public streets was the many peddlers who sold fruits, vegetables, ice, and other items through the streets of Baltimore from their pony-drawn wagons. These entrepreneurs sang their commercials with exuberance:

"Red ripe tomatoes
   delicious cooking apples
Sugar corn
   sure as you born
Sugar corn
   sure as you born"
   and
"Extra, extra
   Here's D. Afro"
   and
"Ice man,
   Ice man,
      Ice man."

These entrepreneurs were enthusiastic about their products and they created celebrative oral and vocal commercials to testify about their belief in them. The imagination of the community was pricked and stimulated. The singing commercials elicited response on the part of the community. Thus, the peddlers and the community benefited.

This street entrepreneurial tradition is similar to the African American preaching tradition. The preachers were always convinced about the value of their product—salvation in this world and salvation in the world to come through Jesus Christ—and they testified in a celebrative way about it. This was done through exhilarating and personal testimonies. They were not objective news reporters; they were subjective proclaimers of what they too had heard, believed, and experienced.

Celebration and Climax in Preaching

African American sermons do not only end in celebration, but the whole sermon itself is celebration. So the meaning of celebration as climax advanced by my mentors and model preachers must be reexamined and extended. I believe that this meaning is too limited. Henry Mitchell said: "We in African American tradition have cultural roots which demand that a sermon *end* in a celebration" (emphasis added).[8] It is true that climax might be that ending portion of the sermon in which phrases and sentences are presented in ascending order in rhetorical forcefulness. Climax ordinarily means, "the final and highest point or the summary explanation among a number of points in the sermon with significant intensity." However, this might or might not be the point of highest celebration of the preacher and audience.

My position is that ending is not the only point of celebration in "good" traditional African American preaching. If celebration means the ecstatic talking and hearing and involvement in the story, then, in most African American sermons, the celebration is interspersed throughout, with greater intensity toward the end. When the African American preacher engages in narration and storytelling with imagination and glorification at several places throughout the proclamation, the preacher and the audience are drawn into an identification with the biblical characters in the story, and the historical event becomes an existential event. Thus, celebration is the natural response.

For example, in the preaching of Manuel Scott Sr. and Sandy Ray, celebration is an ongoing phenomenon throughout their proclamation.

One of Scott's sermons, "The Free Things," was based on a text from the book of Isaiah:

Ho, everyone who thirsts,
    come to the waters;
and you that have no money,
    come, buy and eat!
Come . . .
without money and without price.
    —Isaiah 55:1 (NRSV)

The *free* things, Scott said, are things that cannot wear out under duress of decay. And the *free* things are universally available and are within the reach of everyone. In the outset of the sermon, he began to celebrate these truths and to involve the congregation in the celebration through his poetic use of rhetoric, rhythm, and rests in the movement and presentation of the sermon:

[The Free Things]
    They cannot be isolated by an imperialist
        or taken over by any tyrant.
    They belong to all the centuries

and are the birthright of people
on every continent.
They are God's gracious gifts
to every generation.[9]

I did not hear the proclamation of this sermon, but I have heard Scott on many occasions, and I am persuaded that this was a celebrative portion in this sermon, both in the pulpit and the pew. Remember, one must hear African American preaching in order to appreciate such lines as those above. The practical theological truth that rings out is that God has provided a wellspring of divine blessings and gracious gifts for all people, and no imperialist or tyrant could ultimately block out this eternal birthright.

In his sermon "Melodies in a Strange Land," Ray preached from the biblical text of Psalm 137, and the topic was "How Could We Sing the Lord's Song in a Strange Land?"

At one point in the sermon, Ray told of a time when he had been called to Washington, D.C., along with other leaders, to be told some distressing news about possible dangers in our nation. When he returned home to his pastorate, he said, he was terribly upset, but then he went to a prayer meeting where people were singing, praying, and testifying. A lovely soul came down the aisle, he said, singing "I ain't uneasy, my Lord. I got my ticket bound for glory. I ain't uneasy, my Lord." Sharing this story, Ray testified, "My spirit was lifted." This was a point of celebration in the sermon because his parishioners in Brooklyn, New York, who were captives of the unjust housing, employment, and educational and social systems could sing the Lord's song in this strange and stressing situation. Then the song that this lovely soul led was an epic of hope regularly cited in the African American worship settings, "I ain't uneasy my Lord." Later in the sermon, Ray asserted:

"How shall we sing?"
    We have symphonic souls.
We have chirping, chanting spirits.
    We are on a rhythmic mission.
Singing and praising God
    Cheer us along the weary way.
We sing in strange lands, difficult

situations, cruel circumstances, and
    horrible conditions.
We know that "they that wait upon
    the LORD shall renew their
    strength" (Isaiah 40:31, KJV).[10]

There were four reasons for celebration at this point in the
sermon: One, this revelation was coming in on the wings of
inspiration. The poetic and pictorial style in the presentation
drew the listeners emotionally into the sermon. Two, there was
truth in the statement that related the sermon to the actual
experience of the hearers in their real-life situation. Three, it
picked up an epic from the Old Testament that brought hope
and happiness to the hearts and souls of the preacher and the
people. And, four, practical theological truths were communicated through the preaching. Incidents of celebration in the
preaching included the use of familiar lines and verses, the use
of poetic lines, and the use of repetition, rhythm, and rest in
order to make a point and to involve preacher and listener in
the sermon.

The whole sermon was celebration with rhythmic times of
highs and lows, of fasts and slows, of shouts and whispers, of
intensity and integrity, and never without sincerity and depth
and urgency and spirit.[11] The content of the proclamation was
also a basis for the celebration.

The Content of the Proclamation

It is the kerygma that energizes African American preaching.
In fact, the kerygma is the content of African American preaching. Some may limit kerygma to the Greek meaning of the
proclamation itself or the act of proclaiming. Kerygma *is* the
telling, the authentic announcement or preaching of the Christian message. But it is not limited to the proclamation or the
preaching itself; it is also the content of the proclamation. The
kerygma encompasses all of the promises of the Old Testament
and the historical experiences of the people of God in the Old
Testament. So, when the gospel is preached, the African American can readily experience the kerygma through identification
with God's people of the Old Testament. The kerygma is the
content of the redemption stories as experienced by the Israel-

ites. It is the breaking through of the true eternal and everlasting message. The kerygma is the whole counsel of God. God is Redeemer. Jesus is King of kings and Lord of lords. The Holy Spirit is the empowering presence of God the Father and God the Son. The kerygma does not appeal to the intellect, nor is it understood through any set of propositions. The kerygma—the content of the Christian message—is transmitted from Spirit to spirit through the medium of belief and faith. The kerygma is experienced only through the heart, the soul, and the nature of being.

In the New Testament, the content of the proclamation—the kerygma—is that the promise of redemption in the Old Testament was fulfilled in the life, ministry, death, and resurrection of Jesus Christ. And now God is in Christ reconciling the world to himself.

So the kerygma is the content of the proclamation. The kerygma is *the* Good News. It is central in African American preaching. The kerygma, then, is also the content of the celebration. If the sermon is celebration, there is a substance in the proclamation that elicits the celebration, and that substance is the kerygma.

Practical theology, then, needs to keep a close eye on the celebration so that it can interpret the meaning of the kerygma in every generation. The celebration in preaching, then, will not be merely sound without substance and shouts that are shallow. The celebration will always be the joyful and ecstatic overflow of the hearts of those who proclaim and those who hear and internalize the redemptive melodies in the proclamation.

It is not the act of preaching that leads to the shout or the celebration. It is the content, the "stuff" in the preaching, as comprehended by a people with their backs against the wall, that evokes celebration.

Preaching in the African American tradition took the biblical stories once told, told them again, and made them the testimonies of the preachers and the people in the context of their everyday existence and experience. These stories lost their objective nature and gave way to the subjective belief and experience of preachers and hearers. The preacher would often shift from "he said," "she said," and "it happened" to "I heard," "I feel," "I believe," and "I know." The people would then respond

audibly or inaudibly, "That's right," "That's the way it happened with me," or "I know you're right."

The biblical stories of redemption became their stories
through hearing. These stories gave rise to celebration in
preaching and celebration in the worship experience. Through
these sermons, the people were theologically informed; they
were inspired; and they were empowered to run twice as fast in
order to get half as far, and to work twice as hard to stay there.
They were empowered to endure, to transcend, and to overcome.

The future of African American practical, theological understanding of redemption will depend largely upon the future of
traditional African American preaching. The future of God in
the African American community will depend largely upon the
future of preaching. This will be our focus for the concluding
chapter.

Chapter 8

The Future of the God
We Preach

"Everyone who calls on the name of the Lord shall be saved."
But how are they to call on one in whom they have not believed?
And how are they to believe in one of whom they have never
heard? And how are they to hear without someone to proclaim
him? (Romans 10:13-14, NRSV).

Without a Preacher

To speak of the future of God is not blasphemous. Many gods
were mentioned in the Old Testament: the god of war, the god
of fertility, the god of deliverance, and so forth. In the various
religious communities today, there is the "Jehovah" God, there
is the God of the Trinity, and there is the "Jesus Only" God, all
having some difference in meaning for a particular group. The
future of God, then—how God will be known by the masses in
the future—will depend largely upon the God that we preach.

It was a part of the whole counsel or will or plan of God to
send forth the message of redemption through human beings.
God, in absolute divinity, can do anything, but, by design, God
provided that the medium of the Good News of salvation would
be presented through human creatures. God could have sent the
message through angels. We do have incidents of angelic mes-
sengers recorded in the Bible. God could speak through the
beasts; he spoke through Balaam's donkey (Numbers 22:28-30).
And surely God could speak through material objects: Jesus said
to those who asked him to quiet the shouting crowd as he was
riding into Jerusalem, "I tell you, if these were silent, the stones

would shout out" (Luke 19:40, NRSV).

God, for whatever reason, ordained that the gospel would be sent forth through the preacher; so Paul is right in his rhetorical assertion that they cannot hear without a preacher. I assert, then, with trembling and fear that I might be misunderstood as irreverent, profane, or blasphemous, that the future of the God we preach rests with our responsiveness to the God who calls us to preach. How will the world come to know the love of the living God without a preacher? The God who will be known tomorrow will be the God we preach today. Thus, I speak of the future of the God we preach.

In this age of secularism and relativism, of urbanization and ghettoization, in an ironic way, the future of God is in the hands of the preachers. On the other hand, it is always comforting to know that the future of the preachers is in God's hand. In times of poverty in preaching, God has always raised up a Moses, an Amos, or a John the Baptist. When the liberating aspect of the whole counsel of God was systemically omitted in the preaching among the enslaved African Americans, God raised up plowmen and made them proclaimers and pastors.

God has placed an awesome responsibility upon the preacher. Where there is no preaching, there is no hearing; where there is no hearing, there is no believing; and where there is no believing, there is no salvation, and the preacher is responsible. The preacher does not come in his or her own power but in the power of the Holy Spirit.

The preachers must take heed to God's message to Ezekiel. God told Ezekiel that if he sounded the trumpet of warning and the people did not take heed, their blood would be upon their own heads. However, if Ezekiel saw impending dangers and sounded not the trumpet, then the blood would be upon Ezekiel (Ezekiel 33:1-16). The lesson to preachers here is that the fate of the people is dependent upon the preacher.

The lesson challenges the preachers to be responsive to the task because the people cannot hear without a preacher. Paul clearly understood this responsibility and passed it on to Timothy: ". . . I solemnly urge you: proclaim the message; be persistent whether the time is favorable or unfavorable . . ." (2 Timothy 4:1-2, NRSV). The burden and responsibility rested so heavily upon him that he said to the Corinthians: "If I proclaim the gospel, this gives me no ground for boasting, for an obligation is laid on me, and woe to me if I do not proclaim the gospel!" (1 Corinthians 9:16, NRSV).

This is also the kind of seriousness with which the traditional African American preachers went about their task. They never preached for the sake of preaching. They preached from the conviction that the preacher was the medium and that preaching was the means of communicating the Good News of redemption. They were convinced that this Good News would not get to the people without a preacher.

The Plight of Preaching

In the above-titled sermon preached by Sandy Ray in 1971, Ray declared, "Preaching has become a captive of secularism .... Let us admit that preaching is in trouble." Moving from the negative to the positive, he then told the audience of preachers that a crisis is an opportunity and that they were preaching in the tradition of the prophets:

The prophets and patriots made their marks in history creeping through crises. From Abraham across the Old Testament, these leaders harnessed crises and rode them to dizzy heights of glory.[1]

In spite of the fact that there is a crisis in preaching, crises also provide an opportunity for preaching. Ray asserted that African American preachers have always preached in the tradition of the prophets, who preached through those crises and transformed them into moments of glory. In a bit more than two decades later, we need to hear again that sermon of hope and word of counsel. To be reminded of the tenacity of the African American preachers who stood in the tradition of the prophets will give some encouragement and direction to those who must preach today and tomorrow.

Several impediments stand in the way of African American preaching and practical theology today and in the foreseeable future. One is the coming of young preachers who are not aware of the African American preaching tradition. Another is the problem of preaching by contract rather than by call. Next is the homiletical training that holds up the white preaching tradition as normative. Finally, there is the equating of preaching with any other social vocation.

My observations here are based on my active pastorate of three decades, my service as a teacher and an academic theologian for two decades, and my involvement as president of the United Baptist Missionary Convention of Maryland and board member of the National Baptist Convention, USA.

Let's examine these four impediments that exacerbate the plight of preaching today. First, we do have a number of younger African American preachers coming into the pulpit with little knowledge of the history of and little respect for the African American preaching tradition. The perpetuation of traditional African American preaching cannot be effectively carried out by persons who have not been brought up in the tradition, have not studied the tradition, and have not developed a deep appreciation for the tradition.

Second, the secularization of society is creeping more and more into the churches, and the relationship between pastor and people is becoming more and more a contractual relationship. This is particularly true of my own Baptist denomination. The "package deal" reached through negotiations often seems to be more important than the divine relationship being consummated. Do the pastor and congregation really feel that God is bringing them together, or is this just another business contract, such as that between a baseball player and team owner or any other secular organization?

The responsibility for correcting this malady rests with both preachers and congregations. Some preachers tend to be too concerned with "what's in the package." On the other hand, too many officers and lay leaders of the church have become so secularized that they tend to want to operate the church just as they operate any other business or institution in society. This leads to many problems. The church is not just another business. The church is a divine organism ordained of God, designed to address spiritual and social needs that transcend those of secular society.

One biblical text that trustees, deacons, stewards, and laypersons appeal to when it comes to compensation for the pastor is, "Take no gold, or silver, or copper in your belts, no bag for your journey . . ." (Matthew 10:9-10, NRSV). But the ending of verse

10 reads, ". . . for laborers deserve their food." So these verses are instructive for both pastors and laypeople.

No matter what might be agreed to in the contract—the "package deal"—a relationship that is not based on spirit, trust, faith, and love too often winds up in civil court. It is a sad day in the life of the church when pastor and laypeople must do by *law* what our ancestors did so graciously and effectively by *love*.

This is not to suggest that in the absence of contracts there was an absence of conflicts in the historical African American churches. There were conflicts, but these were often solved in the local church or in the ecclesiastical bodies rather than in the courts as too many cases are today.

Whatever the content of the contract might be today and in the future, the contract ought to be merely the spelling out of the full intent of pastor and laypeople to engage in the redemptive mission of the Master. Where contracts determine relationship and commitment and when courts must settle disputes, preaching and ministries will lose their purpose, efficacy, and vitality.

A third impediment to the future of traditional African American preaching and practical theology has to do with the training of those called to the preaching and pastoral ministry. More African American preachers of the 1990s and the dawning of the twenty-first century will be attending Bible colleges and seminaries. Even the storefront churches today are demanding trained ministers. This is as it should be!

What will be the content, style, and form of the homiletics and preaching courses in the Bible colleges and seminaries attended by these upcoming preachers? First, are preaching and homiletics just as important basic requirements as church history and systematic theology? Second, will the preaching tradition—content, style, and form—of white Americans be normative for the preaching courses? Third, if African American preaching is offered, will it be required or elective? Fourth, will historical African American Bible colleges and seminaries offer preaching courses that are normatively white? The African American preaching tradition has much to offer to the overall preaching tradition. In fact, it just might be the resuscitative instrument for some dying churches around the nation. Some of the white televangelists have already effectively adopted some of the elements in the style of African American preaching.

Required homiletics courses ought to incorporate the best from the black and the white preaching traditions. To be formally trained only in the preaching tradition of the majority culture is an impediment to the future of African American preachers and preaching.

A fourth impediment to the extension of the African American preaching tradition is the apparent lack of seriousness with which some persons seem to go about the task. A word of advice from Sandy Ray is apropos at this point: "Preaching is not a career. Preaching is not an occupation. Preaching is not a vocation. Preaching is not a business. Preaching is a proclamation! It is an act of proclaiming. It is an official public announcement."[2]

How Shall We Preach?

The God who will be known to African Americans in the twenty-first century will be the God whom they encounter through preaching. How, then, shall we preach?

We must preach in the tradition of the masters of African American preaching. First, there must be an all-out attempt to preach the whole counsel, the whole plan and will of God as revealed by God. The preacher must preach the whole counsel of God as revealed in Scripture, in human history, in Jesus Christ, in the Holy Spirit, in the church, and in the social context of existence in the African American experience.

We must seek the finest in the tradition of the masters. The preaching is standing where the fathers and mothers stood. It must convey the kerygma—the eternal truth of redemption—that our ancestors experienced and preached in the African American churches. We must preach from a stance of obedience to the call of God. Like students in a classroom, we must stand up and repeat after our Teacher of teachers in the tradition of our predecessors. And the essence—the kerygma—of the sermon will break through.

African American preaching for the future must be based on practical theology, not just theology for our *heads*, but theology for our *feet*, not just a theology to help the people to know something, but a theology to empower people to *do* something, to participate with God in the plan of realized social redemption in this world as well as eternal redemption in the world to come. The preaching and hearing must aim to become a happening.

Preaching in the future must address people where they are. It must be situational preaching with eternal implications. The preaching opportunity always occurs at the intersection where the human situation of a particular group and the Word of God meet in time and place. The sermon must be true to the text, applicable to life situations, and always relevant to present conditions and to the hope and aspirations of the community being addressed. There must be divine answers to the cries, "What must I do in my particular situation?" just as there are answers to "What must I do to be saved?" Preaching in the African American tradition always responded to both of these questions.

The sermon must be free in style so that there is room for spontaneity under the Holy Spirit, yet it must maintain that aspect of the tradition that keeps the sermon logical, coherent, and in continuity. More and more people are becoming addicted to television. Those who preach for half an hour or so on Sundays must realize that they are addressing the same audience that has spent a week in front of the television viewing logical and coherent plots, stories, and commercials. Free style and spontaneity must be undergirded with coherence and continuity.

The preaching of the masters was bibliocentric. It included elements of reproach, judgment, exhortation, and promise. While the reproach in African American preaching pointed to the sins and shortcomings of persons, it also addressed the corporate sins of an unjust and oppressive social system. The sermons pronounced God's judgment upon persons, upon an unjust society, and upon an unjust nation.

The National Committee of Negro Churchmen (NCNC), discussed in chapter 2, said in its first statement in 1966 that the eruptions, civil disobedience, and violence that were afflicting the nation were the expressions of God's judgment because of the nation's failure to use its abundant resources to enhance the well-being of people at home and abroad.[3]

However, the preaching of reproach and judgment was always tempered with exhortation and promise. Exhortation was the calling upon the people and the nation to adjust and to readjust their lives spiritually and socially in order to achieve a just society. And promise meant preaching hope for the inbreaking of a just society—the coming into a genuine confederation and community of the people of God. One example of this exhortation and hope is found in the first statement of the NCNC. The group called upon the churches to use more of their resources in working for human justice in the places where the "Master" was already at work bringing about social change.[4] There was promise and hope because the participants were assured that the Master was already at work in the redemptive process. This was exhortation; this was promise. This was preaching that was motivating and empowering.

Samuel D. Proctor summarized the African American preaching tradition, which gives directions for how we ought to preach. Four themes that drive his preaching like strong moving pistons, he said, are:

1. God is still present and active in human affairs and intervenes in our behalf.
2. Spiritual renewal and moral wholeness are available to us all.
3. Genuine community is a realizable goal for the human family.
4. Eternity moves through time, and immortality is an ever-present potential. We have already passed from death unto life when we love.[5]

All of these themes are central in African American preaching. The hearers of the first assertion that God acts on our behalf would rightfully apply the "our" to themselves. This is the liberation aspect of redemption.

The third theme having to do with genuine community as a realizable goal was always a major element in the African American preaching tradition. This communal focus looked beyond a society where some people owned all of the means and institutions of production and the others worked for them, or where some people held all of the positions of power and the other people were relegated to positions of powerlessness. The genuine community would fulfill the confederation aspect of redemption. The genuine community would be a community of freedom, justice, and equality. The preachers preached that hope, and the people were empowered to work toward that end. They kept running twice as fast and working twice as hard to reach that goal.

Proctor was correct when he said that often the preacher finds herself or himself in a small and shrinking minority of persons who still believe that a genuine community is possible in America and in the world.[6] But Proctor, as a pastor-theologian, called attention to the promise of God through the prophet Isaiah:

> The wolf shall live with the lamb,
>   the leopard shall lie down with the kid,
> the calf and the lion and the
>   fatling together,
> and a little child shall lead them.
>   —Isaiah 11:6 (NRSV)

Genuine community is possible, and it is possible because it is a divine promise, and that promise is communicated to the people, even in their oppressed situation, through preaching. The preaching is reproach, judgment, exhortation, and promise.

Preaching in the African American community in its most popular and effective form is narrative and storytelling. It is a manner and method of retelling the ancient biblical stories in such a way that they become the living stories of the lives of the listeners.

If we were to follow the tradition of African American preaching, then future preaching would be celebrative in style. Because of the preacher's own conviction, he or she would stand always in a state of holy happiness. The eternal revelation would thus be transmitted through the personality of the preacher in artistic, lively, articulate, imaginative, and poetic style. Thus, the revelation would be transmitted through inspiration and celebration.

How shall we preach? We must preach in the tradition of our ancestors. We must preach the whole counsel of God from a practical theological perspective. The preaching must address the people where they are. It must be bibliocentric. It must be free in style and yet maintain its continuity. One way to assure communication is through narration and storytelling. The preaching must be celebrative, and it should be designed to evoke celebration among the listeners.

Our Future and God's Future

Our future is inextricably tied up in the future of the world. Our world is now a global village, and fewer and fewer people live in isolation from the other peoples of the world. So, when we begin to think about the future, we must think of the future in international terms. As African Americans, and because of the contrivance of social history, we have had to develop our preaching style in social isolation to some extent. But today we are preaching around the world. Any plans for the perpetuation of the African American preaching tradition must be made in light of a worldwide vision.

First, preaching in the future will have to address a highly scientific and technological society. People will be known by numbers rather than personalities. Hopelessness, homelessness, crime, violence, and repression will increase. The sense of worth and selfhood will diminish, and sensitivity to the value and sacredness of human life, which is already in decline, will continue to deteriorate.

Second, urbanization and ghettoization is on the upswing while the percentage of unemployment is going up. The ranks of the poor will accelerate. Sources of income for this new unemployed class are drying up. Thus, urbanization, ghettoization, and lack of employment and income will lead to further family disorganization, despair, crime, and violence. But this is the social context in which preaching will have to take place.

Third, apostasy is setting in. Apostasy in biblical times might be translated today as secularization. There is a tendency toward turning away from the church, an abandonment and defection from previous religious loyalty in the Western world, including America. An editorial in our daily newspaper in Baltimore reported that today Great Britain is largely a secular society. The editorial pointed out that attendance at regular services of the state-supported churches had dropped to a low of 1.1 million. This church-going group is less than 3 percent of the British adult population.[7] We are living through a period of "man come of age," and apostasy or secularism is a real problem for organized religion. Secular ideologies are on the rise. And our theology and preaching will have to address this real context of existence in the Western world.

Contributing to the problems of our future is the further spread of an unjust international economic system. Giant corporations are taking over smaller ones, modernizing and computerizing and rendering human beings expendable. Thus, the rich get richer—having more than they will ever need—while the poor get poorer—not having enough for decent survival. If one travels to Latin America and to the Caribbean and to under-developed countries around the world, one will discover that the giant corporations and the economic means of production are owned by Western giants. One will discover that the workers are largely living at poverty level. One will also discover that manufacturing jobs are leaving the United States, moving to other countries in search of cheap labor. The workers in America are left as unemployed consumers with no resource for con-sumption.

These are some of the emerging problems that will confront us nationally and internationally in the future.

African American practical theology and practical preaching would provide some glimmer of hope for survival and for reform. It would keep people from conforming to a secularized and greedy ideology and give them direction and power to become engaged in the transformation of an unjust social order.

African American practical theology and practical preaching sustained an enslaved people on plantations, empowered them to engage in transformative movements and to achieve first-class citizenship in hamlets and cities throughout this nation in spite of unmovable encumbrances. By its fruits, we can discern its value.

In the myriad of problems affecting our spiritual and social contexts of existence, Jehovah God still has a positive future. In the period of European expansionism, God was the author of the divine rights of kings. The Christian churches operated on what Moltmann described as the "authoritarian principle—God, king and fatherland."[8] The church theologians presented God as the blesser of expansionism and the sanctioner of the dehumanization of peoples around the globe. The oppressors carried out those exploitations under the guise of bringing the Good News of salvation to the heathens.

In America, God was known as the God of "Manifest Des-tiny." This was the movement across the country from the Atlantic to the Pacific, killing and exploiting Native Americans all along the way. This was not in the divine will at all; it was the social policy of imperialistic expansionists.

In North America, a theological position was reached that

God approved of slavery. The conclusion was that it was better to have a Christian slave than to have a free heathen. So practical theology for the slaveholders was to Christianize the slaves but not to set them free. This theological notion was communicated to the masters and slaveholders through the preachers.

In all of the above, the God of Euro-American history was the God who blessed the culture. In the midst of all these fallacies and distortions, African Americans reread the Old and the New Testaments and discovered the God who was the God of redemption—the God of liberation and confederation. They preached a God who was a deliverer and who promised a new community in a new Canaan.

The future of God, then, will depend upon the God we preach. God will either be the God of the "authoritarian principle," who sanctions exploitation and oppression, or God will be the God of redemption who brings liberation and confederation.

If God is the sanctioner of continued exploitation and oppression, then the world is headed for chaos. If God is the God of liberation, the world could be headed for global community, and some semblance of God's kingdom will come on earth as it is in heaven.

The God of the future, however, will not only be the God who is defined through theological treatises in the academy, but the God who is proclaimed to the people in the pew by the pastor-theologians. Examination, preservation, and perpetuation of preaching and practical theology in the African American tradition will be a major factor in the salvation of the world.

Black theology has become and will continue to be a vital element in the African American preaching tradition in spite of secularization, urbanization, ghettoization, and neofundamentalism. Preaching and practical theology from an African American perspective encompass the whole counsel of God, empowering a people with their backs against the wall to participate in God's plan of redemption. This preaching and practical theology is generally communicated in profound celebration. It has been an effective foundation in the African American community, and can be the leaven for the Christian communities in a global context.

What is needed for the future is a commitment from preachers to preach the whole counsel of God. Preachers must be found fruitful. There is an echo coming out of eternity with the question: "... 'Whom shall I send, and who will go for us?' ..." (Isaiah 6:8, NRSV). Pastor-theologians, the answer rests with you, whether black or white, national or international. The future of God depends upon the God that you preach.

Appendix

The Church Responds to the Seventies

Ministers' Seminar
National Baptist Sunday School and Baptist Training Union
Congress, Omaha, Nebraska, June 1970
Lecturer: Sandy F. Ray, Brooklyn, New York
"Spiritual Counsel in Carnal Crises," Acts 27:31

This sermon was preached by the late Reverend Dr. Sandy F. Ray, as noted above.*

I revised the original manuscript, with his permission, to include the spontaneously injected statements from the audiotape. This sermon was included as Appendix I of my dissertation in partial fulfillment of the requirements for my master of divinity degree at Howard University, School of Divinity in 1972.

The original manuscript as preached includes the regular typing that follows. The *italicized* portions of the sermon are the spontaneously injected portions that were not found in the original manuscript. The [bracketed] portions are those that were included in the original manuscript but not in the preached sermon. This is a sermon by a master African American preacher as preached and heard rather than written and read. Editing has been minimal.

—Olin P. Moyd

*The late Dr. Sandy F. Ray was pastor of the Cornerstone Baptist Church in Brooklyn, New York, for thirty-five years. He pastored other churches prior to his going to Cornerstone. He was president of Empire Missionary Baptist Convention for the state of New York. He was also vice president at large of the National Baptist Convention, USA and earned a national and international reputation as a preacher and lecturer.

"Spiritual Counsel in Carnal Crises"

Acts 27:31
by Sandy F. Ray
June 1970

The growing claim of secularism is narrowing the margin of
the spiritual in the minds of many thinkers. *We are becoming so
secular,* and in the mind of a scholar like Harvey Cox, *for instance,*
he at points dwindles the spiritual to fit into a very small
segment of life. "The secularization theory," as pointed out by
Peter Berger, "regards religion as a vanishing leftover from the
dark ages of superstition. This means that those to whom the
supernatural is still a reality find themselves in a status of a
minority." Berger continues that "the spokesman of traditional
religion recognizes this as an age in which the divine has re-
ceded into the background of human concern and consciousness." *And theologians are becoming dangerously secularized, and
many able theologians look unfavorably upon the supernatural. The
"God is dead" concept is very prevalent in our world.*
The church is caught up in this culture in which the spiritual
has a very small margin of operation. The few bases upon which
we have relied are diminishing under the attack by the scruti-
nizing onslaught of secularism. In our personal experiences, we
must discern the mysterious hand of the Almighty, and we must
rely heavily upon the movements of God in history. *We must
make great use of the Bible itself to offset the growing trend of
secularism.*
It is invading the church, and we are doing a great deal of
explaining and dialogue in the pulpit, and there are new people
who are saying instead of having sermons they call the congregations together for dialogue because the crowd is falling off,
and the people don't want to listen to one man tell the story.
They want to participate, and many preachers are using this
method to try to get the crowd out, so that people can participate
in the dialogue rather than in the sermon itself. But you know,
storytelling is more important than dialogue. And where we are
telling a story, if the preacher gets too involved in dialogue, it
becomes a matter of opinion. But when you tell a story, a true
story, there is no dialogue involved in the story. And I think

many of us who, particularly, are not too sophisticated should not get too far off on dialogue and discussion. I think we ought to just tell the story. And one of the things that older preachers did, they could tell the Bible story. And many of our great churches were built up, not on theology really, and we need theology, of course, but they were built up largely on preachers that could tell the Bible story.

Let us lift the apostle Paul out of history and view some of his exciting experiences. We remember him from his early days. He was a young intellectual with great ambition. His zeal led him out upon a reckless mission of persecution of *the early* a small Christian fellowship. He sought and obtained authority to find and bring them to Jerusalem *for persecution and even for death.* Such an achievement would enhance the prestige of this young Pharisee, and ease the threat of those saints. *He had great zeal, the apostle Paul; but Jesus captured his zeal and gave him a decent religion.*

The story of this mission has become one of the most thrilling experiences in Christian literature. That Damascus road incident shocked and reshaped the life of Paul and transformed him from a persecutor to a preacher. His papers of authority from the priests became parchments for missionary notations. His ambitions for leadership in the advanced councils of the church were canceled by a commitment to his Lord: "Lord, what wilt thou have me do?"

I often wondered if Paul ever related his experience to the priest-hood. I often wondered if he ever got a chance to tell his Damascus road experience to the priesthood. He related it quite often. And every time he got in close places he would relate the Damascus road experience. And whenever there were situations in which he was involved that he couldn't quite explain what was happening to him, he would say, "When I was on the road to Damascus . . ." And whenever he told this story, it had something very, very thrilling to do with the life of people. Might I just drop here, I think preachers ought to tell this experience. When we are talking about firstly and secondly and thirdly and in the first place, and in the second place, I think every once in a while we ought to tell about our Damascus road; because we don't testify enough. And we get all involved in theology and the rest of it and many times people don't realize that the preacher has had this kind of experience.

In the twenty-seventh chapter of the Acts of the Apostles is an exiting account of a shipwreck in which the Apostle was involved. He had encountered difficulties with some of the public officials of the Roman Empire. He had appeared before Felix, Festus, and Agrippa. His zeal and sophistication were embarrassing and humiliating to them. The decision was made to send Paul to Rome to appear before Caesar. Paul was considered a threat to the Empire, and his removal was considered strategic for the well being of the system.

When one is considered dangerous to a system, he must either be controlled or liquidated. *And this is what they did in the case of Jesus.* This technique prevails in all areas of our society. This technique has curbed creativity and initiative *on the part of many people* [on the one hand], and encouraged mediocrity on the other *hand.* The world has been advanced by stubborn radicals who had the courage to break over conventional barriers to move our culture *along* [forward].

Mediocrity is the easy way to live. It's easy to get along at the level of a "me-too" type of program. But, to move prophetically, we have to break over barriers, and have to run great risks. Paul took advantage of running the risks; he dared.

It was the feeling of the officials that this radical preacher was responsible for their national difficulties. They were not inclined to examine *their* system. They were dogmatic and totally insensitive to the message of the Christian gospel.

Now, moral and spiritual blindness are always fatal. And most leaders would rather liquidate a radical then to change the system. Most leaders would rather get rid of somebody that was damaging their movement than to look into the movement and see if there were not some possibilities of changing the movement. And this thing moves all through our society. It's not from a local church. And sometimes, if a person is a little radical, the best thing to do is to either harness him or liquidate him.

So, they book the apostle *Paul* on a ship to Rome. On their voyage they came to "Fair Havens" where they lingered for a time, for sailing was terribly dangerous during this season. Paul had advised them to remain even longer, but the centurion listened to the master and the owner of the ship. Paul was a prisoner and a preacher who had no knowledge of navigation. This crisis required the judgement of the sophisticated navigator and experienced pilots, not the impractical speculations of a preacher.

The knowledge of preachers is limited to special areas by most leaders in our society. They are quick to say that whatever the preacher talks about is out of his field. And there is a lot of knowledge that goes to waste that preachers have that many people feel is out of his field to touch situations where life is involved. But God said to Jeremiah, "I have made thee a watchman over the house of Israel." And I want you to be over the house of Israel. I don't want you to run it, but I want you to know what's happening in it. And I don't think the preacher ought to try to run everything in town, but I think the preacher ought to know what's happening in town. And I think his voice ought to be heard prophetically about whatever is going on in the lives of the people.

They launched forth, and a terrible storm fell upon them. For many days, [neither] the sun, moon, nor stars appeared. Paul said, "I warned you, but you are of the opinion that all knowledge is carnal and scientific." There are insights and revelations which escape the test tube, the X-ray, and the microscope. There is an invisible, supernatural empire to which man *has* [may have] access. It is from that empire that I have *my* information. *I have knowledge for which I cannot account. I know some things that I don't know how I know them.* You are practical, but faith *operates beyond the practical. What seems logical and practical can become terribly frightening, but faith goes beyond the logical and beyond the practical. You know, when Simon Peter started to walk the water, his friends told him, "Don't do this." And when he heard the voice of Jesus, he started to get up out of the boat and they cautioned him. They tried to restrain him; they said "Look, look Peter, ah, this is water; it's impractical. It's illogical. Nobody has ever walked water. You are a human being," but Peter said, "Jesus called me." They said, "We know this, but you don't walk on water." And their fears were designed to frighten Peter because they said this is impractical; this is illogical; this has never been done. But Peter said, "Jesus has called me. And when Jesus calls, there is something that strikes me that makes me impractical and illogical, and I'll have to do something that doesn't sound logical and that is certainly impractical. And I'm walking." And the record says he walked the water.*

Brother preachers, if you listen to everybody that tries to restrain you in the many things you try to do in your church, you'll become frightened by the impracticality of things. And there are hundreds of you here today that have done things that people have whispered and said, "Reverend is crazy." "Reverend, you can't take these poor people and do what you're talking about. Reverend, I know these people. These people ain't got the kind of money you're talking about—two hundred thousand and five hundred thousand and a million dollars. Rev, you, you don't know these people." And the preachers listen to a lot of the logical and practical statements of the deacons and of the trustees. A whole lot of what's being done in the church would never be done, but preachers go beyond the logic. And, and, and faith operates beyond the practical. The preacher said, "I'm walking. I heard the voice of Jesus and I never seen anybody walk the water, but Jesus said come. And, and walking this water is not my responsibility. And I'm going."

And then here comes this esoteric language of the apostle.

"You are not going to understand what I'm going to say," Paul says, "for you don't understand this kind of language. You are earthbound, and your knowledge is gadget concealed, concerned, and mine is God concerned, but I've got a message for you: During the storm, during the wind, during the gale, the angel of the Lord, whose I am and whom I serve, stood by me this night. While thunders were rolling, while lightnings were flashing, while winds were blowing, the angel of the Lord, whose I am and whom I serve, stood by me this night. Be of good cheer." Sounds just like a preacher. "Everything's going to be all right." Winds are blowing, ship leaking, storm raging, but the preacher says, "Everything is going to be all right."

"Now you have lost the stern!"

"Rev, what can I do?"

"Everything is going to be all right." ["I have authentic information that our ship is doomed, but there will be no loss of life." "Be of good cheer. . . . for I believe God."]

There were two hundred and seventy-six souls on this ill-fated ship. They were terribly frightened and fatigued. They could sense panic in the eyes of the captain, pilot, and the centurion. They could see that the masters had lost control. They were preparing to abandon the ship, and each one go for himself. But Paul, the preacher, the prisoner, Paul said [spoke to them], "Gentlemen, I started this voyage as a prisoner, but this crisis has plummeted me into the pilot's seat. The hope of your crew has been lost in the storm, but I have a lively hope which penetrates storms."

"In my new role I am prepared to give directives from now on. I was under orders when I left, but I am prepared to give the orders now. I was a prisoner when I left, but, ah, I am pilot now. The Lord has taken out of the hands of the centurions and the captains and the pilots. He has taken the helm and has turned it over to the preacher. I am in charge. There will be no loss of life. I've got a fine technique for survival. It doesn't look that way now when you look at this storm and at this ship breaking apart, but don't quit the ship now; stay with it. There will be no loss of life. Now the ship is going; we are going to lose that. You can almost forget it. If you had any cynical attachment to the ship, forget it. If you've got any important cargo on board, forget it! God is interested in life! God is interested in life! God has told me there would be no loss of life."

"I know that this ship is storm-tossed. These waves are fierce. The roaring thunder seems to shake the everlasting hills. Those terrifying streaks of lightning are threatening. This ship cannot long endure this gale which is upon us. I implore you not to desert the ship at this point." "Except these abide in the ship, ye cannot be saved."

"But Reverend, this ship is in great distress."

"But I have orders from God concerning the preserving of life."

We are indeed in a turbulent period of history. Some of the ships upon which we have relied in the past are in deep trouble. Many of them are no longer sea-worthy. Pilots, masters, and crew are in panic. Many of those on board have sensed the frustrations and helplessness of the pilots and masters of the ship. They feel that the craft is out of hand, and *they* are willing to take their own chance [amid the leaping wave and howling winds], and do the best they can in the storm.

People are losing faith in most of our existing systems and institutions in our society. Youths are losing faith in adults; whites and blacks are losing faith in each other; students are losing faith in teachers; people losing faith in government. We are losing faith because it looks like the ship is sinking, and everybody on board is in panic. And nobody knows exactly what to do now.

This storm represents the shape of our culture. The masters and pilots have ignored the prophets and left "Fair Havens" [at their own risk]. They have depended upon their skill, and *their* science, and *their* computers, and *their* technology, and *their* money, and *their* armies, and *their* bombs, *and in their* diplomacy, etc. They are insensitive to "The rumor of angels." The preacher on board is a star gazer, *they say*. His message is for another world and has no relevance or word to deal with this storm.

"He is a good man, but he does not understand the storm. Paul is a good man, but this is his first voyage of this type. Paul is a good preacher, but he can't deal with navigation." You're wrong, you're wrong, he might not know navigation, but he knows the Navigator. And I would rather know the Navigator than to know navigation.

There is a ship which is sea-worthy. It is built to weather all of the storms of the ages. It has been tested through the centuries. Someone calls it, "The Old Ship of Zion." "She has landed many a thousand." And someone sings, *"there is no danger in the water."* The pilot is the "Captain of salvation." She has hit upon rocks and icebergs. She has been storm-tossed and driven by gales, but she sails on! *Infidels and agnostics, and cynics, and evil men of every generation have assailed her. But she sails on.*

Before our culture crashes in this turbulence, our counsel should shift to spiritual hands. We need pilots to whom angels speak. We need pilots who have had a revolutionary experience on the *Damascus* road to Damascus. We need pilots who can say, "I know whom I have believed, and *am persuaded that* he is able to keep that which I have committed *unto Him against that day* to his hand." We need pilots who can discern life from sinking ship. *The ship is sinking. But God is on board.* We need pilots who defy test tubes and all scientific tests [of mankind]. *We need pilots with soul. We need pilots with ears attuned to heaven.*

I urge the church, *therefore*, to remain on board the ship. There is a competent pilot on board. He is the "Lily of the Valley," blossoming in the dingy ghettos of our cities. He is the Rose of Sharon, "born not to blush unseen and lose its sweetness in the desert air." He is the "Stone cut out of mountains without hands," rolling across the centuries, crushing empires in its wake. He is a "battle ax," cutting his way through the jungles of earth. He is the "Rock of Ages," projecting above the flying dust of the deserts. *He is Wonderful, Counselor, Everlasting Father, Mighty God, and Prince of Peace.*

Remain on board the ship. There are angelic messages in the

night. We may get our highest note of hope while the gale is most severe. Angels move more swiftly during storms. There is an angelic watchman in every storm. There is an angel gazing through all human crisis. *And wherever God's people are, there is an angel cruising in the dark, and you may not see them, but, when trouble rises, God is always there.*

I close Preachers. Preachers *you* must prepare to become pilots. *Because the captains and the pilots and the centurions don't know what to do now.* Our ship of state is in serious distress. You may have boarded the ship as a prisoner, but the crisis demands that you move to the helm. Providence has moved you into a position of authority. You must speak to the panic-stricken masters and hopeless *people* [passengers] on this ill-fated ship. You, preachers, must see *the* glimmers of hope amid the gloom of the crisis. You, preachers, must see this mysterious hand of *the Almighty* God, guiding gales and stabbing these storms. You must have the poise and power to quiet the crew. You, preachers, *must have faith in God and, even while the storm is raging, you must be able to sing* through faith, must see "the storm passing over" with a glorious shout of hallelujah.

It is awfully dark, but the storm is passing over. Nobody can see this but the preacher. Because everybody else is caught in the gale. But you can rise above the storm and above the gale. You can announce to the people down below that the storm is passing over. And I know it's dark right now; I know our world is confused at this hour. And I know we sit today, brother preachers, in the midst of confusion all over the world, but I can rise above it. For I can hear the voice of the Almighty saying the storm is passing over. Hallelujah! Hallelujah! Hallelujah! The storm is passing over. Hallelujah! Go home; go home; go back; go back to your churches. Go back and tell people in doom, in storm, in distress that the storm is passing over. It may be dark right now, but the storm is passing over. I hear the wind blowing. I see the waves as they roll. I see the lightning flashing. But, down in my heart, the storm is passing over. . . . Hallelujah!

Take Hold of the Lifeline
A storm is raging upon the deep,
The wild winds howl and the mad waves leap;
The clouds are hiding the sun from sight,
But the lifeboat's coming and the beacon's bright.

The Pilot stands at the helm to guide
The lifeboat over the waters wide,
When cries from perishing souls come in
Across the reefs and rocks of sin.
The souls that battle with wind and wave
Are crying "We perish! O save, O save!"
They must not call o'er the storm-swept main
For help, from us, and call in vain.
Then haste to rescue each sinking soul!
Lay hold of the oar, tho' the thunder roll!
Where storms are wildest, launch out to save
The helpless ones from a yawning grave.
"The lifeboat's coming! This way!"
The Pilot shouts thro' the storm and cold,
"The lifeline's thrown," I hear Him say—
Take hold, take hold, take hold.

*God bless our hearts. As we walk through the storms of life, there
is a message: The angel of the Lord, whom I serve, stood by me this
night and told me there would be no loss of life. Go back brothers and
let's tell the world, let's tell everybody that angels have been visiting
us. I believe in angels. I believe that God speaks to us in the night and
in the storm. And whatever may be our storms, brothers, just keep
speaking; just keep talking to God, and whatever the critics and
whatever anybody else says, just remember that angels are still talking;
angels are still speaking; God is still saying, "Take hold." And whatever anybody else feels about the storm, I feel in my own heart that the
storm is passing over. Hallelujah!*

Notes

Chapter 1

1. Howard Thurman, *Jesus and the Disinherited* (Nashville: Abingdon Press, 1949), p. 11.

2. James Earl Massey, *Designing the Sermon* (Nashville: Abingdon Press, 1980), p. 17.

3. J. Deotis Roberts, *Black Theology in Dialogue* (Philadelphia: Westminster Press, 1987), p. 84.

4. James H. Cone, *A Black Theology of Liberation: Twentieth Anniversary Edition* (Maryknoll: Orbis Books, 1990), p. xi.

5. Rebecca S. Chopp, "Practical Theology and Liberation," *Formation and Reflection: The Promise of Practical Theology*, ed. Lewis S. Mudge and James N. Poling (Philadelphia: Fortress Press, 1987), p. 130.

6. Henry H. Mitchell, *Black Preaching* (New York: J. B. Lippincott, 1970), p. 203.

7. Henry H. Mitchell, *The Recovery of Preaching* (San Francisco: Harper and Row, 1977), p. 90.

8. Gardner C. Taylor, *How Shall They Preach* (Elgin: Progressive Baptist Publishing House, 1977), p. 24.

9. Carl E. Braaten, *The Whole Counsel of God* (Philadelphia: Fortress Press, 1974), p. ix.

10. Paul Tillich, *Systematic Theology, Book I* (Chicago: University of Chicago Press, 1971), p. 3.

11. Ibid., p. 28.

Chapter 2

1. J. Deotis Roberts, "Black Theology in the Making," *Review and Expositor* 70, no. 3 (1973), p. 330.

2. Roberts, *Dialogue*, p. 7.

3. James H. Cone, *Black Theology and Black Power* (New York: Seabury Press, 1969), p. 5. In his notes on Chapter 1, Cone said Richard Wright used the term "Black Power" as early as 1954 in reference to Africa.

4. Ibid., p. 1.

5. Ibid., p. 6.

6. Stokeley Carmichael and Charles V. Hamilton, *Black Power: The Politics of Liberation in America* (New York: Vintage Books, 1967).

7. Albert B. Cleage Jr., *The Black Messiah* (New York: Sheed and Ward, 1968). The Reverend Albert Cleage was a clergyman of the United Church of Christ and pastor of the Shrine of the Black Madonna in Detroit, Michigan.

8. Carmichael and Hamilton, p. vii.

9. Cleage, p. 4.

10. Ibid., p. 9.

11. Gayraud S. Wilmore and James H. Cone, eds., *Black Theology: A Documentary History, 1966-1979* (Maryknoll: Orbis Books, 1979), p. 23.

12. Ibid.

13. Ibid., p. 24.

14. Ibid., pp. 24-30.

15. Cone, *Black Power*, p. 1.

16. Thurman. The first presentation of the message of this book was at the annual convocation on preaching at the School of Theology of Boston University in 1935. It was titled "Good News for the Disinherited."

17. Benjamin E. Mays, *The Negro's God as Reflected in His Literature* (New York: Atheneum, reprinted 1968).

18. Ibid., "Preface to the Atheneum Edition" by Vincent Harding, p. i.

19. Mays, p. 199.

20. James H. Cone, *A Black Theology of Liberation* (New York: J. B. Lippincott, 1970).

21. J. Deotis Roberts, *Liberation and Reconciliation: A Black Theology* (Philadelphia: Westminster Press, 1971).

22. Wilmore and Cone, *op.cit.* note p. 152, p. 153.

23. Ibid., p. 139.

24. Ibid., p. 144.

25. Ibid., p. 138.

26. Ibid., p. 101.

27. Cone, *Liberation*, p. 23.

28. Roberts, *Liberation*, p. 27.

29. Roberts, *Review and Expositor*, p. 330.

30. J. Deotis Roberts, *Roots of a Black Future: Family and Church* (Philadelphia: Westminster Press, 1980).

31. James H. Cone, *For My People: Black Theology and the Black Church* (Maryknoll: Orbis Books, 1984).

32. Olin P. Moyd, *Redemption in Black Theology* (Valley Forge: Judson Press, 1979), p. 28.

33. Cornel West, *Prophesy Deliverance!: An Afro-American Revolutionary Christianity* (Philadelphia: Westminster Press, 1982), p. 11.

34. C. Eric Lincoln, *The Black Church Since Frazier* (New York:

Schocken Books, 1974).

35. Wyatt Tee Walker, *"Somebody's Calling My Name": Black Sacred Music and Social Change* (Valley Forge: Judson Press, 1979).

36. Harold A. Carter, *The Prayer Tradition of Black People* (Valley Forge: Judson Press, 1976).

37. James D. Tyms, *Spiritual (Religious) Values in the Black Poet* (Washington: University Press of America, 1977).

38. Vincent Harding, *There Is a River: The Black Struggle for Freedom in America* (New York: Vintage Books, 1983).

39. Roberts, *Dialogue*, pp. 28-42.

40. Ibid., p. 104.

41. Ibid., p. 119.

42. Wilmore and Cone, *op.cit.*, pp. 447-48.

43. Ibid., p. 593.

44. Ibid.

45. Ibid., p. 594.

46. Cone, *Liberation Twentieth Edition.*

47. Roberts, *Dialogue*, p. 119.

Chapter 3

1. Sandy F. Ray, "The Church Responds to the Seventies," *Spiritual Counsel in Carnal Crises* sermonic lecture delivered in the ministers' seminar of the National Baptist Congress of Christian Education, National Baptist Convention, USA, Omaha Nebraska, June 1970. Reprinted in appendix.

2. Olin P. Moyd, "Black Preaching: The Style and Design of Dr. Sandy F. Ray" unpublished dissertation in partial fulfillment of the requirements for the master of divinity degree, School of Divinity, Howard University, Washington, D.C., 1972.

3. Tillich, p. 32.

4. Martin Luther King Jr., *Biography of Martin Luther King* (Cambridge: Social Studies Curriculum Program, Education Development Center, 1968), pp. 3-4.

5. Moyd, *Redemption*, pp. 23-24.

6. Martin Luther King Jr., *Strength to Love* (New York: Harper and Row, 1963), pp. 8-15.

7. Ibid., p. 8

8. Ibid.

9. Ibid., pp. 137-138.

10. *Martin Luther King Jr., 1929-1988: An Ebony Picture Biography* (Chicago: Johnson Publishing Co., 1988), pp. 8-9.

11. The National Baptist Convention, USA is the largest African American denomination in this country, numbering eight million communicants.

12. The Reverend Dr. T. J. Jemison led the first major bus boycott in Baton Rouge, Louisiana, in 1953. He was a consultant to Dr. King.

See *Stride Toward Freedom* by Martin Luther King Jr. (New York: Harper Brothers Publishers, 1958), pp. 75-76. Jemison was elected president of the National Baptist Convention, USA in Miami, Florida, on September 10, 1982.

13. Joseph H. Jackson, annual address delivered at the eighty-fifth annual session of the National Baptist Convention, USA in Jacksonville, Florida, on September 9, 1965.

14. Ibid., pp. 8-9.

15. Joseph H. Jackson, annual address delivered at the ninety-seventh annual session of the National Baptist Convention, USA on September 6, 1977, pp. 12-13.

16. Joseph H. Jackson, annual address delivered at the ninety-first annual session of the National Baptist Convention, USA on September 9, 1971, pp. 20-21.

17. Ibid., p. 16.

18. Al Rutledge, "Six major city banks unfairly deny blacks loans," *Baltimore Times*, August 17-23, 1992, pp. 1-2.

19. Massey.

20. Ray, *Spiritual Counsel*.

21. Bruce A. Rosenberg, *The Art of the American Folk Preacher* (New York: Oxford University Press, 1970), p. 96.

22. Ray, *Spiritual Counsel*.

23. Ibid.

Chapter 4

1. Several preachers have discussed this subject of "preaching the whole counsel of God," based on Paul's statement in Acts 20:27, e.g., Braaten's *The Whole Counsel of God*. In *How Shall They Preach*, Taylor included a chapter titled "Preaching the Whole Counsel of God." He said that this subject was in substance the theme used by Dr. George Buttrick in an address to his graduating class at Oberlin Graduate School of Theology "in days long gone by," p. 77.

2. This statement was made by one of my colleagues, the Reverend Dr. Samuel Austin, as we shared an informal conversation on the podium in the ministers' division of the National Baptist Congress of Christian Education held in Pittsburgh, Pennsylvania, June 22-26, 1992. Many adages and proverbs that express profound theological truths flourish in the African American oral tradition.

3. John Fitzgerald Kennedy, inaugural address as president of the United States in Washington, D.C., on January 20, 1961.

4. Jürgen Moltmann, *Theology Today* (London: SMC Press, 1988), pp. 1-4.

5. Ibid., pp. 4-5.

6. Alexander Glennie, *Sermons Preached on Plantations* (Freeport: Books for Libraries Press, 1971), p. iii.

7. Ibid., pp. 21-22.

8. Manuel L. Scott Sr., "The Inviter" in *The Gospel for the Ghetto: Sermons from a Black Pulpit* (Nashville: Broadman Press, 1973), pp. 14-15. Manuel Scott is in much demand as a preacher, particularly in National Baptist Convention, USA pulpits around the nation.

9. Ibid., pp. 15-17.

10. Benjamin Brawley in Mays, p. 153.

11. Caesar A. W. Clark, "The Preacher in the Pastor," ed. William J. Shaw, ministers' division of The National Baptist Congress of Christian Education (Philadelphia: Ministers' Division Publication, 1992), pp. 26-29. This quote was an oral insertion into the sermon as delivered before four thousand ministers and is not found in the manuscript. The Reverend Dr. Caesar Clark has been the pastor of the Good Street Baptist Church in Dallas, Texas, since 1950. He is a national revival preacher averaging thirty weekly revivals a year and has preached forty-eight revivals in one year. He was vice president at large of the National Baptist Convention, USA. His life's story and some of his sermons have been published in David Gray and Helen Gray, *Dr. Caesar Clark: The Man, The Preacher, The Pastor, The Evangelist* (Kansas City: Jesus Loves You Publishing Co., 1982). Many of his sermons have been published in other journals and periodicals.

12. Ibid.

13. Peter T. Forsyth, *Positive Preaching and the Modern Mind* (Grand Rapids: William B. Eerdmans, 1964), p. 55. Quoted by Donald Macleod, *The Problem of Preaching* (Philadelphia: Fortress Press, 1987), pp. 85-86.

14. Clark, p. 26.

15. James Weldon Johnson's poem "The Creation" can be found in *God's Trombones: Seven Negro Sermons in Verse* (New York: Viking Press, 1975), pp. 15-20.

16. William R. Haney, "Communicating Experience with God," sermon preached in the ministers' division of the National Sunday School and Baptist Training Union Congress in San Francisco, California on June 23, 1976. The Reverend Dr. Haney was pastor of the Dexter Avenue Baptist Church in Detroit, Michigan, and a division preacher in the Congress for about two decades.

17. Ibid., p. 10

18. Ibid., p. 11.

19. Ibid., p. 12.

20. Ibid., p. 13.

21. Ibid., p. 15

22. Ibid., p. 17.

23. William R. Haney, "The Promise of God's Presence," National Sunday School and Baptist Training Union Congress (Dallas: June 19, 1973).

24. Ibid., pp. 3-5.

25. Martin Luther King Jr., "I Have a Dream" in Alan H. Monroe and Douglas Ehninger, *Principles and Types of Speech*, sixth edition (Glenview: Scott, Foresman and Co., 1967), p. 463.

Chapter 5

1. Gardner C. Taylor, "A Great New Testament 'I Am'" in *Chariots Aflame* (Nashville: Broadman Press, 1988), pp. 131-140.

2. Ibid., p. 134.

3. Ibid., p. 136.

4. Ibid., "A Human Request and a Divine Reply," pp. 141-150.

5. Ibid., p. 145.

6. Ibid.

7. Ibid., p. 148.

8. S. Leon Whitney, "Shall We Look for Another," sermon delivered at ministers' seminar, National Sunday School and Baptist Training Union Congress in Pittsburgh, Pennsylvania, June 1979.

9. Ibid., p. 4.

10. Ibid.

11. Ibid., p. 7.

12. Ibid., p. 8.

13. This song is still sung occasionally in the African American churches.

14. James Baldwin, *The Fire Next Time* (New York: Dell Publishing Co., 1969), p. 14.

15. Ibid., p. 141.

16. Roberts, *Dialogue*, pp. 53-54.

17. James A. Forbes Jr., *The Holy Spirit and Preaching* (Nashville: Abingdon Press, 1989), p. 15. James Forbes, a friend and colleague in ministry, is a product of the Pentecostal tradition. He was professor of preaching at Union Theological Seminary in New York and is the first African American senior minister of the famed Riverside Church in New York City.

18. Baldwin, p. 58.

Chapter 6

1. Yvonne V. Delk, "Singing the Lord's Song" in *Those Preachin' Women: Sermons by Black Women Preachers*, ed. Ella Pearson Mitchell (Valley Forge: Judson Press, 1985), p. 57.

2. Cecelia Nabrit Adkins, "Just Between Us," *Ninety-Fifty Annual Report* (Nashville: Sunday School Publishing Board, National Baptist Convention, USA, delivered in Atlanta, Georgia, on September 10, 1992), p. 6.

3. Delk, p. 58.

4. Ella Pearson Mitchell, "The Welcome Table" in *Those Preaching Women, Volume 2: More Sermons by Black Women Preachers* (Valley Forge: Judson Press, 1989), pp. 81-87.

5. Ibid., p. 84.
6. Ibid.
7. Samuel Austin, "God and the Black Church," ministers' division of the National Baptist Congress of Christian Education, auxiliary to the National Baptist Convention, USA. An annual publication edited by William J. Shaw. (Philadelphia, 1984), p. 40.
8. I have heard this story told by several preachers, but I have no idea of its origin.
9. T. J. Jemison, annual address delivered at the one hundred-twelfth annual session of the National Baptist Convention, USA in Atlanta, Georgia, on September 10, 1992, pp. 2, 4.
10. Fred B. Craddock, *Preaching* (Nashville: Abingdon Press, 1987), p. 44.
11. J. Alfred Smith, *Preach On!* (Nashville: Broadman Press, 1984), p. 15.
12. I first discussed these elements of black preaching in my unpublished dissertation for my master of divinity degree. See note 2, chapter 3.
13. John Illo, "The Rhetoric of Malcolm X" *The Columbia University Forum* 59, no. 2 (1966), pp. 5-12.
14. Ray, *Spiritual Counsel.*
15. Ibid.
16. Ibid.
17. Henry H. Mitchell, *Black Preaching*, p. 15.
18. Ray, *Spiritual Counsel.*
19. Louis E. Lomax, *The Negro Revolt* (New York: Harper and Row, 1962), pp. 90-91.
20. Ray, *Spiritual Counsel.*
21. Massey, p. 20.
22. Martha Jean Simmons, "Women for Such a Time as This" in *Women: To Preach or Not to Preach*, ed. Ella Pearson Mitchell (Valley Forge: Judson Press, 1991), p. 80.
23. Ibid.
24. Thomas H. Groome, "Theology on Our Feet: A Revisionist Pedagogy for Healing the Gap between Academia and Ecclesia" in *Formation and Reflection*, pp. 62-63.
25. Shirley Virginia Knight Budd, "Go Back and Wait!" in *Those Preaching Women, Volume 2*, pp. 21-27.
26. Ibid., p. 23.
27. King, p. 463.

Chapter 7

1. E. Franklin Frazier, *The Negro Church in America* (New York: Schocken Books, 1969), p. 13.
2. Henry H. Mitchell, *Black Preaching*, p. 81.
3. Joseph R. Washington Jr., *Black Religion: The Negro and Christianity in the United States* (Boston: Beacon Press, 1969), pp. 42-43.

    4. Ralph Wiley, *Why Black People Tend to Shout* (New York: Penguin Books, 1991), p. 1.

    5. Ibid., p. 2.

    6. This is one line from the song "Keep So Busy Working for My Jesus."

    7. Gloria Gerald, "I Had to Tell Somebody" in *Women: To Preach or Not*, pp. 49-50.

    8. Henry H. Mitchell, *Celebration and Experience in Preaching* (Nashville: Abingdon Press, 1991), p. 12.

    9. Manuel L. Scott Sr., "The Free Things" in *Gospel for the Ghetto*, p. 32.

    10. Sandy F. Ray, "Melodies in a Strange Land," in *Journeying through a Jungle*, ed. W. Franklin Richardson (Nashville: Broadman Press, 1979), pp. 55-63.

    11. The rhythmic inserting of highs and lows, shouts and whispers are regularly incorporated in the preaching of Frederick G. Sampson, pastor of the Tabernacle Baptist Church in Detroit, Michigan.

Chapter 8

    1. Sandy F. Ray "The Plight of Preaching" a sermon delivered in the ministers' seminar of the National Baptist Congress of Christian Education in Little Rock, Arkansas, in June 1971, p. 2-4.

    2. Ibid., p. 4.

    3. Wilmore and Cone, p. 24.

    4. Ibid., p. 27.

    5. Samuel D. Proctor *"How Shall They Hear?"* (Valley Forge: Judson Press, 1992), p. 10.

    6. Ibid., p. 55.

    7. "Women and the Bishops," editorial, *The Sun*, November 19, 1992), p. 18A.

    8. Moltmann, p. 4.